THE NEW HERO

Ronald Sutherland

Essays in Comparative Quebec/Canadian Literature

THE NEW HERO

Macmillan of Canada / Toronto

ISBN 0-7705-1613-0

Canadian Cataloguing in Publication Data

Sutherland, Ronald, 1933–
    The new hero

Bibliography: p.
Includes index.
ISBN 0-7705-1613-0 pa.

1. Canadian fiction – 20th century – History
and criticism. I. Title.

PS8187.S86   C813'.5'409   C77-001685-5
PR9192.5.S86

Printed in Canada for
The Macmillan Company of Canada Limited
70 Bond Street
Toronto, Ontario   M5B 1X3

Contents

*For both JANETS — the aunt who raised me
with love and wisdom, and my first daughter,
for whom I am trying to do the same*

*I am once again grateful to my friend
Cormac Gerard Cappon for his expert assistance
in proofreading this book.*

Introduction

When my first volume of interrelated essays, *Second Image*, was published in 1971, the field of comparative Canadian literature was still relatively unexplored, and I felt obliged to define and to elaborate at considerable length, to map out the territory, as it were. Over the past few years, however, comparative studies of English-Canadian and Quebec literature have proliferated, opening up many new vistas for those interested in the totality of the Canadian literary experience. This book, therefore, although a sequel to *Second Image*, is not so exclusively devoted to the basic issues and broad implications of comparative analysis. Some essays deal with specific authors, works, or subjects because of their intrinsic interest, such as the Second World War as seen by Canadian writers or the humour of monologuist Yvon Deschamps.

The conclusion formulated in *Second Image* is that English-speaking and French-speaking Canadians have a great deal in common, that they share a single mystique, and *The New Hero* will serve to corroborate that conclusion, especially with regard to the emergence of the "new Canadian hero". The notion that the two main language groups of Canada should have anything in common, incidentally, appears to be, as I learned from certain reactions to *Second Image*, anathema for some people. It is now the custom among Quebec writers and critics to refer to *la littérature québécoise*, but there are a few *littérateurs* who absurdly feel that changing the name makes it an exclusive preserve which would somehow be contaminated by the traditional comparative approach applied by scholars to all national literatures since the ancient Greek. Choice of terminology, of course, is a matter of personal preference, and considering the pejorative connotations which have come to be associated with *canadien-français*, I see good reason why *littérature québécoise* should be used, and *littérature acadienne* or *black American literature* for that matter. These terms are precise, appropriate, and presumably acceptable to all.

But regardless of what it is called, Quebec writing, by force of history and circumstances, is not really divorced from the rest of Canadian literature, however much anyone might wish that it were. Limited knowledge or ignorance of one or the other, or of both, does permit the illusion of dissimilarity; but those who have read widely in both bodies of literature know that the major Quebec writers demonstrably share the distinctive themes and subject matter treated by Canadians who write in English. Novelists of the land and divine order such as Hémon, Guèvremont, and Ringuet, for instance, have more in common with Grove, Ostenso, and Knister than with contemporary Quebec authors such as Aquin, Carrier, or Godbout, and there is no way to change that fact. Actually, the three modern writers mentioned have little in common with each other except language, and even then their styles are quite divergent. Which is as it should be — Canada has become a far more complex society than it was in the first half of the century, providing a wide variety of themes and subject matter, and authors in all parts of the country have become more experimental and individualistic. In other words, that there should be differences among individual writers, whether francophone or anglophone, is hardly a notable phenomenon. Of course there are differences. In any book-writing nation there are differences. By pointing out that Quebec and English-Canadian literature have a number of basic themes in common, I am not suggesting that distinctive qualities do not exist. What I do contend, however, is that when the writing of the two major language groups of Canada, despite long isolation and determined efforts to insulate, nevertheless reveals a spectrum of shared values and attitudes, then whether one likes it or not that phenomenon is of far greater significance than the normal and expected differences.

The well-known actress Micheline Lanctôt, who is now living in Los Angeles for purposes of her career but who is nevertheless a strong supporter of Quebec independence, illustrates the point clearly and succinctly. In an interview for the December 1976 issue of the magazine *l'Actualité*, she was asked: "Comment voyez-vous le Canada et le Québec, de là-bas?" — *How do you see Canada and Quebec from down there?*

Lanctôt's reply:

> J'ai découvert toutes sortes de choses, là-bas. Comme le fait que le Canada anglais n'est pas américain. Ici, on croit toujours qu'il n'y a pas de différence. Et il y en a une énorme. Ils sont beaucoup plus près de nous. Quand on rencontre un Canadien, ça clique tout de suite. Il y a une personnalité de base qui est canadienne. . . . (p. 10)

When you meet an English Canadian, something clicks right away. There is a basic Canadian personality. But Micheline Lanctôt, like myself, would hardly suggest that there are no differences. She is simply impressed, as I and others have been, by the discovery of a fundamental similarity.

A subject which is examined at some length and in several contexts in this volume, the nature of social culture, is the key to these similarities and differences. Culture in a society is the set of values and mores which conditions the individual's reaction to the world around him and which provides him with a sense of identity. In any society, culture has different levels or layers, like coats of paint on a wall. The first layer is applied by the immediate family during a person's infancy, then subsequent layers form as the individual moves out into ever-widening social circles, the number of layers depending on the individual's opportunity and desire to enlarge his horizon. Arrested cultural development, the root-cause of prejudices, feuds, racism, and chauvinism, occurs when new layers stop forming at an early stage, so that the individual is incapable of seeing beyond his own backyard.

Writers perforce must draw upon their various layers of cultural consciousness when they work, and the writing which has the greatest universal significance derives of necessity from the earliest or latest layers of cultural conditioning; that is to say, from the basic human inner-circle experiences or from the broad philosophical issues which concern all mankind. Canadian writers are no different from other men of letters. Those whose works probe the inner circle of a human being's relations with other human beings or the outer layer of man's relationship to the universe are bound to strike common chords, not only with each other but with good writers throughout the world. Both the differences and parallels which exist among Canadian authors, francophone and anglophone, depend upon the layers of culture from which their works are predominantly distilled. When authors like Ringuet and Grove, for example, explored the psyche of the farmer in Quebec and the prairies, they discovered identical attitudes toward the land, hardship, sex, and the duty to conform to a particular divine plan, indicating that, despite superficial cultural differences, there were levels where the values of a certain class of Canadians coincided. The same coincidence can be seen in the novels of Gabrielle Roy, Hugh MacLennan, Jean Simard, and Adele Wiseman, to mention just a few of the writers who examine Canadians trying to adapt to urban living,

Canadians who have obvious cultural differences. Indeed, it is precisely because of the obvious cultural variations that the common levels are significant. Today, as the first essay in this volume will illustrate, there are still such levels. And in the long run, I am sure, analysis of this intriguing phenomenon and its implications will provide greater insight into the social realities of both French and English Canada than extolling the qualities of writing encased in its own idiosyncrasies.

The essays in this volume are essentially "para-literary", meaning that they examine literature from the viewpoint of social realism and thus often spill over into the areas of psychology, sociology, philosophy, economics, and history. The last, history, especially invites attention, for Canadian writers in both English and French are now in the process of a serious re-evaluation of the past. In Quebec, even comedians such as Yvon Deschamps are busily engaged in dismantling many of the hallowed myths and traditions of days gone by, as will be seen in the essay on Deschamps in this book. The historians themselves are doing much the same thing, and entirely new concepts of Canadian history are emerging.

I have always had sympathy for the historian, who, it seems to me, is confronted with a dilemma — either he can be objective and scientific and run the risk of being dull and unreadable, or he can be exciting and inspirational at the expense of objectivity and accuracy. Canada has had its share of both kinds of historians, and my impression is that the scientific and dull ones have predominated in English Canada, while the inspirational and exciting have, at least until the last few years, *mené le bal* in Quebec.

My impression, of course, need not be taken as anything more than that — an impression. But there does seem to be something amiss with the image of English Canadians, a layer of cultural conditioning where they differ from their French-speaking compatriots. Not long ago in the American magazine *National Lampoon* there was a little joke on English Canadians. It went like this:

"Did you hear the one about the Canadian and the farmer's daughter?"
"No, what happened?"
"He married her."

Now obviously the French-speaking Canadian also married the farmer's daughter, but in order to get to the ceremony, as the Quebec historian used to see it, he had to trudge through a howling blizzard, cross a river on drifting ice, climb a mountain and fight off a pack of wolves, escape hunting parties of Indians and Orangemen, then be led the last ten miles to the church by an angel of God hovering in the air before him. In other words, written history and literature have been intertwined in Quebec. Much of the historical writing has been highly imaginative, while a good deal of the fiction writing has been historical and close to reality, sometimes too close to reality (in the cases of Albert Laberge and Jean-Charles Harvey, for instance) to avoid the censure of the ecclesiastical authorities.

Perhaps Lord Durham was right. His famous remark about a "people without a history or a literature" was what motivated François-Xavier Garneau to become a historian and Philippe Aubert de Gaspé to become a novelist. But Durham also observed — a remark not nearly so well-known in English Canada — that French Canadians were more cultivated, more refined, and more capable of speculative thought than their English-speaking compatriots. And certainly a number of Quebec historians have not gone out of their way to prove him wrong, exhibiting in fact a considerable capacity for speculative thought.

The pattern was set by historian Garneau and novelist Aubert de Gaspé. Garneau's pioneering *Histoire du Canada* in three volumes is a remarkable work in many respects — inspirational, lofty — but it is the novelist Aubert de Gaspé in his *Les Anciens Canadiens* who left us fascinating and detailed descriptions of the Quebec of his youth. The clergymen historians, among them Jean-Baptiste Ferland, Etienne-Marcel Faillon, Henri-Raymond Casgrain, and Canon Lionel Groulx, were all inclined to adapt history to their own convictions, religious or otherwise. Canon Groulx, to be sure, was the most influential in articulating the themes of nationalism in Quebec. He used history as a weapon, as an instrument to communicate his own philosophy, including some pretty unsavoury notions on race. And the process continues today, despite the fact that a group of highly competent historians are at work and many excellent volumes are being produced. An example of history as a weapon or vehicle in our own day is Léandre Bergeron's *Petit manuel d'histoire du Québec*, which has reputedly sold more than 75,000 copies. It has also done well in comic-book form, which might be an idea for the publishers of Lower, Careless, and Creighton to investigate.

But I do not mean to be disparaging about the historian who superimposes his own idea on his subject matter. The myth-makers are important and necessary. If, however, I were advising someone on what to read to know the history of Quebec, I would definitely include the novelists and poets as recorders and interpreters of reality, both social and psychological. I would suggest works like *Maria Chapdelaine, Trente Arpents, Bonheur d'occasion, La Bagarre,* and *Prochain épisode,* all of which are examined closely in either this volume or *Second Image.* In these novels the reader would relive some of Quebec history, he would feel what certain generations of Québécois have felt rather than be told what ideally they should have felt. He would see the influence of the myth-making historians such as Garneau and Groulx in the erstwhile sense of mission and attachment to *notre maître le passé* dramatized in *Maria Chapdelaine.* Ringuet's *Trente Arpents* depicts the breakup of the Quebec rural order, and *Bonheur d'occasion* goes a step further, studying the displaced people in the slums of the big city. Bessette's *La Bagarre* illustrates changing attitudes toward the church, morality, education, and labour relations, while in a book like Hubert Aquin's *Prochain épisode* the reader experiences the frustration and desperation of many young people in contemporary Quebec.

To my mind, then, history and literature are complementary. With some historians, those who stray furthest away from the strict presentation of documented fact, the two fields overlap; such historians are creative writers. I believe that the scientific, objective historian is necessary — he collects, sorts out, and presents the facts about our past which help us to understand ourselves. But the other kind of historian, the one who uses history as a vehicle for his own philosophy, is equally necessary. It is he, along with the creators of literature, who helps to build the myths which become the sustaining force of any culture. Man cannot live by facts alone. Nor are truth and reality sufficient to provide a *raison d'être.* Pretence is the defence of the sober and sensitive against the emptiness of demonstrable truth.

I must add, however, that while I think that the scientific historian and the creative historian and writer are necessary for any society, it is essential to have both, so that they may counterbalance each other. The myth-maker may sometimes turn into a propagandist, distorting and deforming in the interests of mind control. It was Paul Valéry who wrote: "History is the most dangerous product which the chemistry of the intellect has elaborated."

In both English and French Canada today, there are the necessary counterbalances. One of the reasons is simply that writing has greatly increased in quantity and variety, reducing the possibility of single dominant figures. But a more important reason, as this volume will demonstrate, is the change in attitude, the new independence of mind being exhibited by contemporary Canadians. Neither the French-speaking nor the English-speaking people of this country are as gullible and trusting as they used to be. There is general recognition of the fact that the difference between the factual and fictional writer, between the scientific historian and the novelist, is not one of subject matter but rather of degree of artistic involvement. The creative writer expressly allows his imagination full play; he tries to shape his raw materials into an artistic whole. If he is a good writer, he does not deform or falsify — he simply shapes. The factual writer, the objective historian, is less artistically involved. He may arrange, but presumably he does not shape his materials. Who, then, arrives at the greatest truth? I should think that it depends upon the individual writer.

Moreover, there are different kinds of truth. A poet and a historian are talking together, and the poet mentions a girl he knew many years ago. He especially remembers one June night, when he and the girl were sitting on the old swing behind the house. The lilacs were in full bloom and the air was heavy with their delicate fragrance. In the soft moonlight flickering through the leaves of the trees she ran her hand over the hair he used to have and whispered, "Johnny, I love you." She was the most beautiful girl in the world, recalls the poet.

But the historian, being the sort of man he is, cannot accept that statement. He does a little research. School records show that the girl was ten pounds overweight and had trouble with her left eye, which was slightly crossed from birth. Old order slips at the local pharmacy reveal that she used to buy a lot of brewer's yeast and elastic stockings, indicating that she had skin problems and varicose veins. There can be no doubt that she dyed her hair. A trip to the dentist's office provides proof that she had 20 per cent more cavities, probably bad breath besides. She could hardly have been even an attractive girl, let alone the most beautiful girl in the world. The poet is wrong.

But then again, maybe he is right. His truth is one of feeling rather than fact, and feeling can often be more vital than fact. Life without poetry is a drab business. It is bad enough that hockey has gone down the drain. In Quebec, Saturday-night hockey used to be as much an integral part of life as eating, drinking, and trying to effect the revenge of the cradle. But because of commercialism, greed, and expansion, not anymore. When the Russian poet Yevtushenko was visiting Canada, someone asked him who was his favourite Canadian poet. "Phil Esposito," he replied, and perhaps he touched upon a greater truth than he realized. With non-international hockey essentially dead, a lot of the poetry has gone out of the lives of the people of Canada, and of Quebec in particular.

Along with the poetry, a lot of the magic and mystery of old Quebec are going too. In English Canada, as will be seen in the essay on Robertson Davies in this book, it is not so much that these qualities have gone but the realization that they were always denied that hurts. Mastering the past instead of being mastered by it, healthy as the process may be in the long run, inevitably has the effect of demystification, removing the protective covering of mystery and sacredness. It is almost like discovering proof that the mother you adored cheated on the father you respected. So you must go through a period of angry readjustment, tossing out the old furniture and mementoes, burning the album with the yellowing photographs, even throwing the old portrait of papa into the flames.

Canada, as can be seen in the works of so many current writers, is going through such a period of angry readjustment. The traditional St-Jean Baptiste Day Parade in Quebec is an interesting case in point. From the time of the original colony there has been a celebration on June 24, the feast day of the patron saint of Quebec. Generally the parade featured a cherubic, blue-eyed, curly-haired child riding the last float with his arm around a terrified white lamb. In 1963, pressures were successfully brought to bear to get rid of the lamb, which, it was argued, might be construed to symbolize Quebec. A tiger would be better, but it might take a notion to eat the little boy. Then a compromise was struck — sculptor Gaétan Therrien produced an eleven-foot papier-mâché statue, which he himself described as "strong, powerful, dynamic", and in 1964 the statue replaced the curly-headed child. Despite its aura of strength, however, the statue did not survive the St-Jean Baptiste riot in 1968, when Prime Minister Pierre Trudeau was on the reviewing stand. Unable to get at Trudeau, who remained on the platform defiantly, the frustrated mob toppled and decapitated the statue of St-Jean. Alleged relics of the missing head of the saint were passed around Montreal for weeks afterwards. And there has not been an official St-Jean Baptiste Day Parade in Montreal since.

But only the parade has been discontinued — the celebrations have gone on. In 1975 there was a five-day party on top of Mount Royal with hundreds of top professional artists, a veritable show-piece of Quebec culture. More than a million people climbed the mountain to take part in the festivities, and they included thousands from the Italian, Greek, English, Ukrainian, Haitian, and other ethnic communities of the metropolis and province. Collectively, thus, the Québécois added a new and significant cultural layer. And despite the sharp break with tradition, it was in effect a return to a distant and misty past, to the celebration of the Summer Solstice and the zenith of the sun by the ancient Gauls, the event which was trans-formed into the Feast of John the Baptist by the Christian Church. In other words, there was a jumping over of the immediate, some-what xenophobic past to an older, tribal past, and to something shared by many tribes.

The essays in this volume attempt to illustrate that the same process is taking place in wide areas of contemporary Canadian life and being reflected in Canadian literature in English and French. The present is being manhandled and the past is being reassessed, to be sure, but a new confidence and a new image are being created, and the future may well reveal that the current demystification has led to older, deeper, and greater mysteries which transcend the barriers of language and ethnic culture.

NOTE ON TEXT PRESENTATION

All page references in this volume are to the editions listed in the Bibliography.

With a view to preserving as much as possible the full flavour of quotations from works in French, while at the same time not requiring the reader to be bilingual, I have adopted a two-sided policy. Single lines and short passages not likely to be misunderstood by anyone with a knowledge of school French are left in the original. Long passages and expressions in colloquial diction or otherwise likely to present problems for those who are not fluent in French, are given in my own translation, while the original texts are retained in the footnotes.

1.
The New Hero

A few years ago, during the surcharge controversy between the United States and Canada, one bright commentator managed to ease the tensions with a humorous story. The American president, he said, after carefully studying some old treaties and maps had come to the conclusion that Detroit and Chicago were actually located on Canadian territory. And if Canadians did not stop complaining about the surcharge, the story went on, the United States of America would be forced to make Canada take Detroit and Chicago back.

In fact, however, as Canadians well know, there have been many permanent and temporary transfers of people, territory, and jurisdiction between the United States and the remainder of North America over the past two centuries. From 1894 to 1919, for example, Canadian immigration policy was virtually dictated by the American government, with U.S. officials stationed at Canada's ports of entry. At another time, *la belle ville de Montréal* was an American city. On November 13, 1775, rebel troops under General Richard Montgomery, formerly an officer in the British Army, entered Montreal unresisted at the old Récollet Gate. One of the twelve prominent citizens who signed the statement of capitulation was a man called James McGill, a fur-trader with grandiose dreams of founding an "institution of higher learning".

The American occupation of Montreal, of course, did not last long. French Canadians, their loyalty to the British Crown possibly stirred by the church's threat of excommunication, did not flock to the rebel cause as the Americans had anticipated. Americans have never been good at anticipating loyalties. By June 1776, Montgomery had been killed in the assault on Quebec City and the Yankees had gone home.

An intriguing aspect of the whole affair, however, is the remark made by General Montgomery on the distinguishing characteristics of Americans and Canadians, or at least of the progenitors of Americans and Canadians. Apparently the General found a vast difference "between commanding the disciplined troops of the British

Army and the independent, truculent, insubordinate Yankees of the revolutionary Army". As historian Andrew Collard phrased it: "His men might be willing to consider his commands. Whether they would obey them or not was their own decision."[1]

Two hundred years ago, then, certain national traits of Canadians and Americans were already beginning to sprout, and what is important to us now is that these traits as they blossomed and took on definition became powerful conditioning forces in American and Canadian culture and literature. Comparative examination of the two literatures, American on the one hand and Canadian writing in both English and French on the other, provides illuminating insights into the evolution of the two sets of cultural values. In the United States, as a succession of best-sellers such as *The Greening of America* and *Future Shock* have underlined, society has fragmented, and values are in a state of disintegration, transmogrification, or nostalgic goal-line stands. And in Canada lately, seemingly in the last five or ten years, cultural evolution has also taken some dramatic twists, producing among other things a new type of Canadian hero, a phenomenon which could well be of profound significance. Before confronting the new hero, however, it is expedient to define the old hero by recapitulating briefly the major values reflected in American and Canadian literature up to the 1960s and 1970s.

Both Canada and the United States, as we know, were strongly influenced by Puritanism, but the Puritan ethos developed quite differently in each country, and an understanding of this difference is to my mind still the key to understanding the evolution and import of both literatures. The effect of Puritanism on American thought has been well documented and needs no further commentary. In Canada, the Calvinistic doctrine also prevailed, both among Protestants — Scottish Presbyterianism being especially strong — and among Roman Catholics — Jansenism, or *Rigorisme* as it is sometimes called in French Canada, conditioning both Irish and French Catholicism. But while Americans and Canadians had the Puritan ethos in common, as I illustrated in *Second Image*, there were significant divergences in emphasis and interpretation.

The major Puritan thinkers of the United States, Jonathan Edwards in particular, put far more stress on the depravity of man than apparently did their Canadian counterparts. What is more important, however, is that American Puritanism, developing as it did from the peculiar notions of a small and persecuted sect, underlined self-reliance and the responsibility of the individual. In reaction to the idea of an established church, there was an aversion to any hierarchical, centralized, or extensively structured church system. Canada, by contrast, had relatively sophisticated church systems among both Catholics and Protestants. New England Puritanism and subsequent evangelical movements called for personal seeking of God, working out one's own salvation through "fear and trembling". Canadians, on the other hand, had the security of reliance upon a church establishment, detailed codes of behaviour, a controlling system; and in general, *until very recently*, Canadians have tended to depend upon and to trust systems which control their lives, whether religious, governmental, social, educational, or of late, labour union.

The labour unions, incidentally, have now become the arena of a great deal of the energy of nationalism in Canada. Groups of locals are attempting to break away from foreign control, which now they see as sending dues out of the country in the face of disinterest in regional problems on the part of an absentee leadership. In Quebec, the unions have jumped into the vacuum created by the steady recession of the church as a controlling force. Yet the Quebecker of the 1970s — and I believe that the phenomenon is closely related to the emergence of the new hero — is not as trusting as he used to be. Workers have occasionally defied labour leaders, some of whom seem more interested in power than in the welfare of their charges. Confusion has arisen with respect to Quebec independence. Some labour leaders who on the one hand demand wage parity with Americans or more, thus presupposing economic integration and expansion on a continental scale, on the other hand call for the separation of Quebec, which presupposes at least a temporary shrinking of the regional economy. Otherwise, it would obviously be necessary to induce a heavy influx of foreign-investment capital to maintain the illusion of prosperity, making independence a hollow gesture. Of course, no Quebec leader of any sort could hope to survive if he were to tell his supporters, as did Fidel Castro, that they must tighten their belts.

But to get back to Canadian Puritanism, it was less extreme than the American variety, colouring life in greys rather than in black and white, which explains why Canadian literature did not have a Melville or a Hawthorne. Nor did Canada have a Benjamin Franklin, the man who split American Puritanism in two, adopting the principles of industry, efficiency, self-reliance, and success as a signal of God's grace, then dropping God from the picture to create the rationale of American materialism. Meanwhile, Edwards went to the other extreme, tormenting himself with the impossible task of harmonizing dark Calvinism with enlightened rationalism, and inaugurating a tradition of highly disciplined intellectualism. This tradition, too, soon dropped the old Puritan God, had already done so by the time of Emerson and Thoreau, but it has retained an obsession with ethics. The American artist-intellectual tradition, in reaction to the conformism of the materialist stream, elevated and glorified the principle of self-reliant individualism.

Tension between the two poles of individualism and conformism, the basic American dichotomy, has informed all the literary classics of the United States from *Moby Dick* and *Huckleberry Finn* to *As I Lay Dying* and *One Flew over the Cuckoo's Nest*. A sobering thought, perhaps, is that the self-reliant individualist in American fiction, once the ideal and the winner, is now becoming the loser. In *Cuckoo's Nest*, the protagonist McMurphy, possibly the toughest individualist of them all, is finally crushed by a regimented system.

Now in Canadian fiction, until very recently, the protagonists, in sharp contrast to the pre-Kesey American hero, were not only losers but determined losers. Canadian literature has never been conditioned by tension between two poles. Often enough to be sure, there was confrontation between the individual and the system (whether religious, social, or other), but seldom conflict. Because of the conditioning force of the peculiar Canadian Calvinist-Jansenist tradition, when a protagonist discovered that he was in disagreement with the dictates of the system, instead of defying it or fighting it as do American protagonists from Hester Prynne to McMurphy, the Canadian protagonist blamed himself. The tension thus used to become internalized, the character engaging in painful and destructive soul-searching in an attempt to discover his own deficiencies. Falling precisely into this category are the heroes of most Canadian fiction of any note before 1970 — the novels of Hugh MacLennan, Morley Callaghan, and Margaret Laurence (partially), Frederick Philip Grove's *Settlers of the Marsh*, Sinclair Ross's *As for Me and My House*, André Langevin's *Poussière sur la ville*, and Hubert Aquin's *Prochain épisode* are but a sampling.

Viewing the main bodies of American and Canadian literature side by side, then, the salient differentiating feature is in the attitudes of the protagonists. The American is defiant, hurling challenges not only at the system but sometimes even in the face of God. The pre-1970s Canadian is self-effacing, struggling within himself to find an accommodation of some sort. This difference in attitudes is the result of the divergent devolutions of the Puritan ethos in each country, the glorification of individualism and self-reliance on the one side and trust in authority and systems on the other. I should point out, however, that other factors are involved, and certainly there are other interpretations. In her book *Survival*, just as Frederick Turner and Henry Nash Smith once claimed the idea of the frontier to have conditioned American thought and literature, Margaret Atwood makes a case for survival as a conditioning concept in Canada. But like the frontier, survival explains only partially, and it is perhaps too general a notion to have particular bearing. It could indeed be applied to any literature and traditionally characterizes the stance of the artist or sensitive person in relation to a stifling environment — Darl in *As I Lay Dying*, Hamlet, Madame Bovary, various characters in Chekhov, Ibsen, D. H. Lawrence, Hardy, Chinua Achebe, Richard Rive, Naipaul, and George Lamming come immediately to mind. Northrop Frye is more specific when he speaks of the garrison mentality of English Canadians, and D. G. Jones, who has the advantage of knowing the literature of both English and French Canada, sees Canadian writers as conditioned by certain myths and as the creators of a peculiar Job-Jonah-like mythology of their own. To my mind, each of these overviews is accurate according to its own terms, and more often than not the differences among them are in terminology rather than substance. Certainly each has contributed to an understanding of Canadian literature, but it still seems to me that each must perforce be an aspect or offshoot of the major religious conditioning force, the distinctive Calvinist-Jansenist rationale of Canada.

Historical events and traditional values of the United States and Canada, as we know, are closely connected with each nation's interpretation, either conscious or unconscious, of the Puritan ethos. American scholars have explored the development and effect of such positive myths as "Manifest Destiny" and "Garden of the World" and have shown how they are related to the Pilgrim notions of a divine mission. Even the rise of capitalism has been linked to the distinctive American Protestant ethic. In Canada, what myths did develop — the "Revenge of the Cradle" in Quebec, for example — were generally regional, and the absence of all-embracing positive myths had the effect of keeping the affirmation of "Canadianism" low-keyed. On the other hand, the ultra-positive character of American myths, the "American Dream" if you wish, has led to bitter disillusionment reflected in the writings of Irving and Cooper to Fitzgerald, Mailer, and the black authors of the twentieth century. In the long run, having expected less and received perhaps more than they expected, contemporary Canadians may be psychologically better off than Americans, and it could be an awareness of this state that is being reflected in the most recent Canadian fiction.

Whatever the case, it is clear that the themes which can be used to categorize American literature do not apply to the body of Canadian writing. As I outlined in a previous study,[2] major Canadian works of fiction fall into three general thematic divisions: 1) The Land and Divine Order; 2) The Breakup of the Old Order; and 3) The Search for Vital Truth. And each of these divisions ultimately relates back to the Calvinist-Jansenist world view.

To some extent there is a parallel between Canadian works in the "Breakup of the Old Order" category and American works which treat the disintegration of the American dream. The important distinction, however, is that the American character – in Miller, Fitzgerald, Salinger, and Baldwin for instance – is disillusioned, and he blames the nation, society, the system for cheating him. In keeping with the Canadian Calvinist-Jansenist tradition, the Canadian protagonist is not disillusioned, at least not in the same way. Rather he is confused, and more often than not he suffers from a guilt complex. The Old Order is falling apart, the old values do not seem to make sense any more, and the Canadian character blames himself for his disbelief. After all, the system, the values are far greater than he is. He has not been, like the American, seasoned in self-reliance and individualism and distrust of authority. He cannot sincerely say with Henry David Thoreau, "That government governs best which governs not at all."

Some of the authors who deal with the "Breakup", notably MacLennan in *The Watch That Ends the Night*, Simard in *Mon fils pourtant heureux*, and McDougall in *Execution*, find an answer to the disappearance of traditional values in a philosophical posture which can be called "realistic involvement" — accepting life as it is with all its miseries and absurdities, but still retaining the capacity to love others and to struggle for whatever small improvements are possible. But there is no suggestion that somehow Canada as a nation implanted a false dream, made promises that were empty, cheated the individual in any way. Instead the Canadian character simply concludes that God's design is not what it was cracked up to be, that he can no longer depend upon the old values and the system. Accordingly, he learns that he must depend more upon his own resources; in other words, he must develop the legendary American virtue of self-reliance. But not for the reasons expounded by the New England Puritans, Benjamin Franklin, or the Transcendentalists, not to make himself an exhibit of the grace of an ever-watchful divinity or even a vessel for the spirit of the Oversoul. Rather he must become self-reliant because God is not really interested in him any more and he is on his own. He cannot, therefore, become self-righteous about either himself or his nation.

It is now evident that the heroes of the "realistic involvement" novels in the "Breakup of the Old Order" thematic division foreshadow the emergence of the new Canadian hero. Between these works of the 1950s and those of the 1970s there is the whole series of novels characterized by the "Search for Vital Truth", novels which present heroes for whom the traditional values mean nothing at all. They are not sorry about their inability to adapt, nor are they intent upon making an accommodation. These characters begin at zero; they have no values, and they are searching for some kind of *raison d'être*. For some of the protagonists in Quebec fiction the idea of an independent nation — separatism — provides a temporary direction. But even the revolutionaries in Aquin's *Prochain épisode*, Jasmin's *Ethel et le terroriste*, or Gravel's *A perte de temps* do not find the cause sufficient to provide a life direction. The protagonist of each book is confused to begin with, and then he becomes even more confused. It is a big leap from the Calvinist-Jansenist total-life-controlling Old Order to a state of nothingness. For some writers the personal *raison d'être* of their characters is tied up with the *raison d'être* of the nation itself, a questioning of whether Canada does, can, or should exist as a nation. And it seems to me that no major American writer, even the most disillusioned black poet or novelist, has had quite the same sentiment. American writers question and lament what the United States has become, to be sure; they call for changes, revitalization, and rededication, or else they despair that the deterioration is too far advanced, but never do they question their nation's existence or their own identity as Americans, however much they may resent both. Even Ralph Ellison's "invisible man" knows who he is — his problem is that others (white Americans) do not really see him.

The Canadian writer in general, however, is not especially burdened by his "Canadianness". The regional or tribal identity is the largest factor in the group consciousness of most Canadians, and the implications of pan-Canadianism can simply be ignored, which, as Hallvard Dahlie demonstrates in an article in *Canadian Literature*,[3] is exactly what happens in many recent Canadian novels. In fact, as I have intimated, a number of remarkable things are happening in the novels of the last two or three years. Particularly illuminating is to examine the leap from one of the old thematic divisions to a new one — "Discovery of Vital Truth" — in the writings of single authors who have published over a long period. Sinclair Ross, Adele Wiseman, and André Langevin have all brought out new works in 1974, Ross's *Sawbones Memorial* appearing thirty-three years after *As for Me and My House* and Wiseman's *Crackpot* coming eighteen years after her brilliant novel *The Sacrifice*. André Langevin's best-known work, *Poussière sur la ville* (translated as *Dust over the City*), appeared in 1953, more than two decades before *Une Chaîne dans le parc*.

Ross's *As for Me and My House* stands as a prime example of the old Canadian hero and the Calvinist-Jansenist rationale. Philip Bentley, the protagonist, is presented from the viewpoint of his wife, who is the narrator of the novel. Bentley is a clergyman, and for many years he carries on a ministry in which he does not really believe. Typically, he lacks the self-confidence and individualism to break away, to defy the system, and he spends his time sitting at his desk sketching people without faces and the false store fronts of a little prairie town. When eventually his frustration and circumstances combine to lead him to the seduction of an infatuated and equally frustrated choir girl, the act is not a grand passion, nor even an expression of affection or physical desire. Rather it is a foolish, desperate, self-punishing gesture. Bentley's struggle is thus internalized, as is always the case with novels of the "Breakup". The Old Order, no longer the life-directing force illustrated in the fiction of the "Land and Divine Order", still remains as a hangover. The certainty is gone, and the uncertainty torments. Characters in the first thematic category suffered, but they believed that they knew why and that life's afflictions were a guarantee of eternal paradise. Philip Bentley does not know, and the cross he bears is his doubt.

The protagonist of Sinclair Ross's latest novel, *Sawbones Memorial*, is a complete and intriguing contrast to Philip Bentley, even though he is also a professional man in a small prairie town. "Sawbones" Hunter is a country doctor retiring at the age of seventy-five after nearly half a century of practice. The town has finally built a hospital, which will be known as the Hunter Memorial, but it will be in the charge of a young doctor. A local boy, Dr. Nick Miller is still familiarly referred to by many as "Nick the Hunky". His mother was a Ukrainian charwoman known as Big Anna.

Doc Hunter has never been able to adapt to the system, the code of behaviour and attitudes expected of a doctor by the general public. Actually, he has simply ignored the system, doing his job and living his life in his own way, despite the gossip about his drinking and womanizing. Unlike Philip Bentley, he is self-confident, self-reliant, and individualistic, even to the point of making personal, non-medical decisions which govern the very lives and deaths of people around him. When asked by the local newspaper editor if he ever had any doubts, Hunter replies, "If anything ever kept me awake it was for having hesitated, held back, not the other way" (p. 113). On one occasion he performed what amounted to euthanasia for a farm woman in the final stages of cancer. On another, when a father killed with a pitchfork a man who had attempted to rape his daughter, Doc Hunter declined to inform the police, deciding that justice had been done and that a court case would only cause needless suffering for all: "Back in town after I'd signed the death certificate — after I'd faked it, in fact — it struck me that without batting an eye I'd taken it on myself to be judge too. What we call the normal process of law — why bother? Wasn't Doc Hunter doing all right? I suppose you could say I've always had a practical, commonsense way of looking at things — even a fairly decent way" (p. 115). On still another occasion, Doc Hunter aborted a young girl who was pregnant by her father, then managed to rehabilitate both the man and his daughter.

Hunter, thus, is astonishingly different from the stolid, God-fearing, unbending patriarchal heroes of Canadian novels of the "Land and Divine Order" or from the guilt-ridden, tormented protagonists of the "Breakup of the Old Order". Like Philip Bentley in Ross's earlier novel, Doc Hunter has an illegitimate child. But instead of the child becoming a symbol of guilt and misery, Hunter's son is his triumph. When Big Anna, who came to clean the Hunter home, said "You vant?" he took without hesitation. Then he kept tabs on the boy as Anna raised him, paying the bills, smoothing his way in the community, taking him along on his doctor's rounds. The reason that Doc Hunter has no regrets upon leaving Upward when at last a hospital has been built, is not only that he is satisfied with himself and his long career, but also that his practice and the hospital will be, as Doc alone now knows, in the hands of his own son — Nick.

Hunter, it seems, has never had an internal struggle with himself. Questioned by the local clergyman about his philosophy respecting life and moral issues, he replies: "Long ago I gave up trying to make anything of them. As you say, I've been a practising doctor; my time has been pretty well taken up with the practical problems of the job." Hunter believes in a divinity, but he does not subscribe to the divine design of the Old Order — "An intelligence, yes. A purpose or plan, I'm not convinced." When the clergyman presses him further, Hunter uses the analogy of Dr. Ehrlich's discovery of a cure for syphilis, a compound of arsenic called 606 because it was the result of the 606th experiment. Hunter thinks of the world as an experiment, but not the 606th one which proved to be successful. The world as we know it is a failed experiment, "maybe 8 or 9 — or let's be optimistic, coming along in the 400s. Or maybe much closer, nearly there — 601, 605. . . ." The world, accordingly, has been discarded: "No help and no interference either. Strictly on our own — sink or swim in our infested mud-bottomed little Here and Now. The odds, I suppose, not very good, but still you never know . . ." (p. 128).

Believing that he is on his own, therefore, Doc Hunter must be self-reliant and independent. One is tempted to say that he is more like an American than a Canadian, especially when he is taking the law into his own hands. In fact, however, Hunter is quite Canadian, perhaps peculiarly Canadian. Although he is obviously listening to his own drummer, he presumes no transcendental metronome to set the beat of his drum, and he is symbolic of the total escape from the trammels of the Calvinist-Jansenist Old Order. American Puritanism contained the seeds of its own destruction and transformation; Canadian Puritanism simply eroded, leaving a memory rather than a mutation. Doc Hunter is independent and self-reliant not because of prescribed and inculcated national values, but rather in spite of them. His life is not an act of traditional defiance, but of submission, submission to his own instincts, and of "realistic involvement" without the soul-searching and anxiety. There have, in fact, always been Doc Hunters in Canadian fiction, but they were never the respected heroes. They were outcasts and renegades like the Ben in W. O. Mitchell's *Who Has Seen the Wind*, Madeleine in *Poussière sur la ville*, or Jerome in *The Watch That Ends the Night*. What has happened in Canadian fiction is that the erstwhile outcasts have suddenly become the heroes. Now that the Old Order and the conventions of society have faded away, those who managed to live outside the pale have become the subjects of intense examination.

We always knew that they were there, despised them, marvelled at them, and pitied them, but now we would like to know their secret, their vital truths.

The Judaic version of the Old Order is powerfully illustrated in Adele Wiseman's *The Sacrifice*, probably the best Jewish novel written in North America. But like Sinclair Ross, Wiseman has published another novel which this time has a remarkable individualist as protagonist. Abraham in *The Sacrifice* struggles to obey the code of an orthodox Jew, and his life is given epic proportions in the novel. He tries to accept his lot, including the murder in a pogrom of two sons, and the deaths of his wife and his remaining son in Canada, but finally the pressures become too great. Not that he turns against God and His design however. In a demented state he thinks himself the instrument of God's design and commits a murder, finally to be incarcerated in an asylum.

The protagonist of Wiseman's latest novel, *Crackpot*, is also Jewish, the fruit of a bizarre, ritualistic marriage between a blind man and a hump-backed woman. During a time of plague in Russia, when the Christians appeared to be stricken more severely than members of the Jewish community, there was danger of a pogrom arising to add to the threat of the disease itself. The Jews were thus forced to take action to "restore the forces of life when only the forces of death reigned before". The traditional rite was to take the two poorest and most helpless members of the community, a man and a woman, and stage a wedding in a cemetery. The community provided a dowry, a hut for the couple, and also undertook to look after them. Thus it came about that Danile and Rahel, the parents of Wiseman's heroine, Hoda, were joined in marriage. Then eventually they found themselves in Winnipeg, supposedly to be cared for by Danile's uncle. The uncle, however, was tricked — he did not realize that Danile and Rahel were handicapped when he agreed to sponsor them. His insulting remarks and resentment lead the two immigrants to attempt to support themselves, Rahel working as a charwoman and Danile weaving baskets. When Rahel dies, Uncle Nate offers to put both Danile and Hoda into institutions, but they resist, preferring to be independent and to look after themselves as best they can. Danile, of course, cannot manage alone, but he has absolute faith in the providence of God's design. The burden of actually providing falls on the broad shoulders of his daughter.

Big for her age and grossly overweight, Hoda does housework as her mother had done before her, but she soon finds out that there

are easier ways for a girl to make money. The local butcher gives
her scraps of meat and soupbones in return for small sexual favours,
and it is not long before Hoda slips into friendly, neighbourhood
whoring. She pretends to her sightless father that she is tutoring the
boys who come to her home; he repeatedly calls out to them in
Hebrew to study (occasionally causing discomfort "because the
word for 'study' in Hebrew sounds like the word for 'pig' in Yiddish").
Hoda is a large, boisterous girl full of good cheer, and she prospers
as a whore; at least she earns enough to keep the ship afloat. Early in
her career, before she becomes really professional, she gets pregnant,
but she is so fat normally that she does not realize she is with child
until the last moment. Wiseman is at her descriptive best in the
scene where Hoda gives birth, then wrapping herself and the infant
deposits it at the door of a Jewish orphanage.

The climax of the book, again a masterful piece of writing to
handle a scene which boggles the imagination, comes when Hoda's
own son turns up with a group of youths to sample her services, and
to pay the treat with money his unknown mother has secretly been
sending him! The first time he is with her she does not know that
he is her son, but after she has realized the truth, he wants her again.
Understandably, Hoda is shaken:

> *Tell him! Tell him now!* Tell him? After the contempt he hadn't been
> able to hide when she tried to hint? Tell him, sure; give him something
> to be proud of. How to make happy a miserable little boy. Oh sure,
> tell him. "*Say, you know what? I just remembered. I AM your . . .*"
> Sure, go on, tell him, after what's happened already too, what happened
> earlier on tonight, before you knew, that you keep trying to forget.
> *Well that wasn't my fault; I didn't know. I couldn't help it.* (p. 246)

It is highly significant that Hoda is not beset by feelings of guilt,
only remorse. In order to spare the boy the knowledge that his
mother is a whore, a notorious whore known to the whole community, she suppresses her natural desire to claim her son. In fact,
she allows him to sleep with her a second time, again to spare his
feelings.

Like Doc Hunter, Hoda has been too busy with day-to-day working and living to become preoccupied with the philosophical issues
of life. Like Hunter, she is tough when she has to be, but she is
essentially good, genuinely concerned about others to the disregard
of her own interests. She is also self-confident and self-reliant, capable
of turning aside insults and cruel allusions and of ignoring the

system. She has only vague notions of conventional morality, speculating alternatively that what feels good must be right or that what feels good must be wrong, but she is never overly concerned. The Old Order, which coloured every moment of the life of Abraham in *The Sacrifice*, does not operate for Hoda. It is something in the stories told by her blind father, old meanings in an old country, an abandoned experiment. Once again, the "American" virtues are not prescribed, but are simply a reaction to the invalidity of the traditional values with respect to the practical business of living.

What then sustains people like Doc Hunter and Hoda? Obviously they do not regard life as either a purgatory to prepare them for future paradise or a divine pattern to fulfill, as do characters of the "Land and Divine Order". Why do they not fall apart as do so many of the characters in the "Breakup" novels? Why in particular does Hoda, whose life is punctuated with sordid experiences crowned by incest, not become demoralized like the prostitutes in other Canadian works of fiction — Callaghan's *Such Is My Beloved*, Garner's *Cabbagetown*, Grove's *The Yoke of Life*, for instance? The explanation, clearly, is that Doc Hunter and Hoda do not develop guilt complexes. Expecting paradise neither here nor hereafter, they have nothing to lose. And a vital truth which both have instinctively acquired is the capacity to love and to be emotionally involved with other people. In a way, then, they do practise the "realistic involvement" mentioned earlier, with the distinction, however, that unlike the characters in the earlier novels, they have not engaged in painful internal struggle and philosophical debate to arrive finally at the position. They are neither existentialists nor losers in the game of life.

Now as might be expected from the previous parallel thematic development of English-Canadian and Quebec literature, the new hero has found expression in both languages at the same time. Moreover, there is the additional parallel of a single prominent author who once was known as the creator of a prototype of the old hero, abruptly coming forth with a model of the new hero.

The protagonist of André Langevin's 1953 novel, *Poussière sur la ville*, is the epitome of a determined, self-punishing loser. Doctor Alain Dubois is possibly even more perverse than Wiseman's Abraham or Ross's Bentley, purposely sitting in his darkened office to listen to the giggles and groans and squeaking of springs as his pretty wife services another man in the living room. *Une Chaîne dans le parc*, like *Crackpot* and *Sawbones* published in 1974, tells an entirely different kind of story, about a boy called Pierrot who is brought up in an orphanage. The novel covers a short period when Pierrot is living with an uncle and three aunts in central Montreal, after he has become too old for the orphanage. It does not take long for the relatives to decide to send Pierrot to another institution, a live-in trade school. Their reason, evidently, is that the boy is too independent and self-reliant for them to handle.

And there can be no doubt that Pierrot is a budding Doc Hunter rather than a Doctor Dubois. Despite his orphanage training with nuns ("les corneilles" — *the crows*), he insists on making up his own mind, even in matters of religion. When asked by one of the local youths ("le Rat") if he believes in God, Pierrot replies: "Ça, je sais pas. C'est plus difficile. J'aime mieux croire à . . . en quelqu'un d'autre." — *That I dunno. Hard to say. I prefer to believe in somebody else* (p. 34). Like Hoda and Hunter, Pierrot does not trouble himself with questions of ethics. After he has been kicked by "le Rat", we are told: "L'idée ne lui vient pas de lui demander pourquoi il lui a donné ce coup de pied, parce qu'il n'a jamais cherché à savoir pourquoi il recevait des coups." — *It does not occur to him to ask why he has been kicked, because he has never tried to figure out why he was being hit* (p. 25).

Pierrot is an active boy and ready to fight furiously for what he believes to be his rights. He can no more be pushed around than Doc Hunter (who confiscates livestock for his fee when justified) or big Hoda (who pulls a mountie off his horse during the Winnipeg strike). Even as a child at the orphanage Pierrot breaks the nose of a bully ("le grand Justin") who has been tormenting him for a long time. Yet he has sympathy and understanding for other people, including Gaston "le Rat": "Les chiens, c'est pas leur faute; ils sont faits pour mordre. Gaston, c'est pareil." — *Dogs, it's not their fault, they can't help biting. The same with Gaston* (p. 38). And certainly he becomes emotionally involved with Jane, the pretty and precocious child who lives with her prostitute mother in the flat next to that of Pierrot's uncle.

But Pierrot absolutely refuses to occupy himself with exaggerated or unjustified feelings of guilt. When his uncle commands him to ask pardon for disturbing his Aunt Maria, he says: "Je lui demanderai pas pardon, parce qu'elle m'aime pas sans même m'avoir connu. . . ." — *I will not apologize, because she doesn't like me and she doesn't even know me* (p. 53). His aunts take him to the cemetery where his mother is buried and use all their devices to make him feel sorry and somehow responsible for her death. But Pierrot resists:

All of a sudden he does begin to cry, without having felt that the tears were coming, but it is from rage against his aunts, their stage performance, their way of being old and living, their dragging him there as if he were guilty himself, or were taking somebody else's place, their acting like saints when they were incapable of talking about anyone without skinning him alive.[4]

Pierrot's relationship with Jane is highly revealing. She has long blonde hair (from her English-Canadian father?) and wears expensive, dainty dresses (compensation from a mother whose profession leaves her with not much loving to spare). Pierrot, straight from the orphanage, has only vague notions of the difference between boys and girls, but he finds Jane attractive and magnetic. Acting on his impulses, he defies his aunts and Jane's mother. He even defies "le Rat" to become the little girl's companion and protector. The two children, of course, are too young to accomplish sexual union, despite the more sophisticated Jane's efforts, but they do find joy in each other's company. Pierrot remains self-reliant and strongly independent — "J'irai où je voudrai. Et si vous n'êtes pas contentes, je m'en irai." — *I'll go where I want. And if you don't like it, I'll leave* (p. 120). — enjoying the companionship while at the same time realizing Jane's shortcomings. Actually, Jane is like a young Madeleine, the wife of Alain Dubois in *Poussière sur la ville*. She is a wild thing, all sensuality and physical appetite. At one time Pierrot speculates "qu'elle est gourmande, non seulement de la bouche, mais de tout son corps." — *that she's a glutton, not only with her mouth but with her whole body*. At ten, Pierrot seems to understand more about the opposite sex than Dubois does as a grown man. Or at least he is more capable of acting upon what he knows.

Toward the end of his short period of liberty from institutions, Pierrot's experience has taught him that there are two general categories of people:

He understands that there is the tribe of those who refuse to submit themselves, like everybody else, to that which is expected of them and which is decided upon by he does not know whom, another tribe, much more numerous, wearing jackets and ties, educated and lacking pride, who go to work every day in the same place for twenty, thirty years, who accord the greatest importance to the severed heads of kings disguised as ordinary heads on money and do not even notice how a marble tints the sun with such beautiful colors.[5]

Pierrot decides that he is a member of the first tribe, the individualists who go their own ways. Likewise, of course, are Hoda and Doc Hunter, and all three are dramatizations of the new Canadian hero.

Another, perhaps more spectacular (although not completely resolved) example of the new hero occurs in yet a fourth novel published in 1974, Adrien Thério's *La Colère du père*. This work tells how the Bishop of Rimouski decides to build a new church to replace the old chapel erected by the first settlers of the area. Gaudiose Martel, head of the large Martel clan, is sentimentally attached to the chapel and does not want it replaced. When the fat Bishop, with the full authority of his office, insists, an incredible event occurs, incredible at least according to the Jansenist Old Order of Quebec. The Martels, following their chieftain, become Protestants and engage a minister to preach in the pioneer chapel.

The new hero, thus, has suddenly exploded from the pages of Canadian fiction. The character type has always been there, lurking in the work of Margaret Laurence (then coming finally to full bloom in the course of her excellent novel *The Diviners* — another 1974 publication), Hugh MacLennan, W. O. Mitchell, and others, but not fully developed, or else keeping out of the way, playing a secondary role. Now he is the main character playing the dominant role, and he is not the end-product of a long struggle with himself. He is strong, self-reliant, self-trusting, confident, and highly individualistic, but unlike the legendary American hero of similar traits, he is not the self-righteous exponent of established national values. He is respected, however grudgingly at times, without being respectable in the conventional sense. Actually, he seems to operate outside the scope of respectability. Undoubtedly he reflects changes now taking place in Canadian society, the new attitudes commented upon earlier in this essay. Representing a profound transformation in the very image of Canadians, the implications of the new Canadian hero could be far-reaching indeed.

2.
Tabernacles à Douze Étages

Nationalism is a loaded term. To different people it has come to mean different things, some of them pleasant but many of them unpleasant. It can be the harmless euphoria produced across this country when Yvan Cournoyer scored the tying goal and Paul Henderson the winner in the final moments of the first Canada-Russia hockey series. But it is also associated with racism, hatred, war, and destruction, with the ruthlessness of Nazi Germany, with Arab terrorism, with the intransigent attitudes of various Israelis, Irishmen, Americans, and Canadians, among others. In short, the energies generated by nationalism can be enormous and blinding. Seeking only a place in the sun, they can reap the raging blizzard.

Nationalism as we know it today, moreover, is not necessarily a phenomenon confined to a political nation according to the established concept. Within large nations there are ethnic groups frantically trying to maintain or to create distinctive cultural identities. And cultural identity, of course, is a matter of vital importance, for it has to do with human dignity and basic attitudes toward life. Expanding communications, as well as trade and travel, have immensely enlarged man's consciousness of the world around him and of important events everywhere, moving us closer in many respects to Marshall McLuhan's "global village". At the same time, advances in communication and the rapid development of giant international corporations have vastly improved the opportunities for cultural domination by the more powerful and dynamic nations of the world, without benefit of old-style colonization and the river gunboat. Nowadays the process is far more subtle and efficient. The spread of the American way of life — Coca-Cola, quick lunches, Playboy bunny clubs, supermarkets, the lifetime goal of a chicken in the pot and a car in the garage — provides the obvious example, an example of which Canadians are acutely aware. The opposite trend, the nationalistic urge for a singular and distinguishing cultural identity, is seen among the emerging new nations of the world and among ethnic groups — Welsh, Scots, Bretons, Bengalis,

Basques, an estimated 6,000-strong group of Gaelic-speaking Cape Bretoners, Crees, Inuit, Québécois, and Acadians. Canadians know something about that too.

In fact, by dint of circumstances Canada has become a microcosm of the contemporary trends mentioned above, an arena for the play of various centripetal and certrifugal forces. And there are some who appear to feel that, as W. B. Yeats wrote in "The Second Coming" — "The falcon cannot hear the falconer;/ Things fall apart; the centre cannot hold."

It seems to me, however, that in order to comprehend the situation in Canada today, the patterns of thought reflected in a good deal of Canadian writing, one must begin with an analysis of the very nature of nationalism and its relationship to culture. Exactly what is nationalism? What are its implications for Canada? In his controversial volume, *Without Marx or Jesus,* French scholar Jean-François Revel writes of the "cultural colonization of European urban life by U.S. values, language and patterns of behaviour".[6] He goes on to say that the European elite have lost their ability to initiate or to define; they "no longer feel at ease as anything but disciples." Revel argues that the new philosophy involves the death of nationalism and the establishment of world government. Now if nationalism is dead or dying in Europe, and certainly there is some truth to Revel's thesis, then why is it blossoming forth in Canada? Could it be that if Europeans "no longer feel at ease as anything but disciples", the opposite is now true in Canada? Have Canadians decided that they are no longer willing to accept the role of disciple? How is all of this related to the emergence of the new Canadian hero?

But to return to our inquiry into the precise nature of nationalism, dictionaries supply only the vaguest of definitions. According to the *Standard College Dictionary,* for instance, it is "Devotion, often chauvinistic, to one's own nation and to its political and economic interests or aspirations, social and cultural traditions, etc." The "et cetera", incidentally, is an actual part of the dictionary definition, permitting limitless possibilities and precluding any degree of precision. Moreover, the nature of nationalism obviously depends upon what one understands by the word "nation". It is possible, nevertheless, to discern two distinct kinds of nationalism. The first I call *political* nationalism, and the second *cultural* nationalism.

Political nationalism is based upon the concept of a political nation, such as the U.S.S.R., Spain, or Nigeria. Cultural nationalism, on the other hand, derives from the kinship feelings of a cultural or

ethnic group, such as the Ukrainians or Lithuanians in the U.S.S.R.,
the Basques in Spain, or the Biafrans in Nigeria. Clearly then,
political nationalism is more superficial than cultural nationalism.
It would also appear that it is generally the more malevolent and
sinister of the two. Whereas cultural nationalism is rooted in the
ethnic group's desire to survive, to preserve an identity, to maintain
a set of values and attitudes which produce feelings of belonging,
security, and dignity, political nationalism is seemingly rooted in the
desire to expand and to dominate — in short, the desire for power.
There is no need to provide examples. Simply consider the history
of Europe in the nineteenth and twentieth centuries, or the
nationalistic madness which helped to bring about two world wars.
There are occasions, of course, when political and cultural nationalism
coincide, or at least appear to coincide. The modern state of Israel is
an example, although perhaps not the best, for I understand that
many cultural problems are still to be resolved there. More often, it
would appear, political nationalism is the mortal enemy of cultural
nationalism. The larger political entity attempts to suppress the
ethnic group, or at least to toss it into the melting pot. Political
nationalism can even bring about the voluntary abnegation of
cultural nationalism, as grotesquely illustrated by those who
accepted to be "honorary Aryans" during the Second World War.
Political nationalism, furthermore, is at once the father and the child
of the propaganda machine; no man needs to be taught that he is a
member of an ethnic group, but he may need to be conditioned to
be a "good" citizen of a nation. While cultural nationalism seeks to
expand the individual's freedom to realize himself, albeit within
a defined context, the political variety often seeks to suppress that
freedom. Accordingly, from the point of view of the human condition,
it can be said that generally cultural nationalism is a positive factor
and political nationalism negative.

Now in Canada, obviously both political and cultural nationalism
have existed and exist today, and both have found expression in
Canadian literature. Undoubtedly, however, political nationalism
has in the past played a relatively secondary role, and the history of
Canada explains why. The absence of positive national myths in this
country has been commented upon by a number of writers. New
France, to be sure, had inspirational, positive myths, but they were
shattered by the Conquest. The Loyalists, also defeated, took their
inspiration from fidelity to the Crown of England. The dreamers, the
myth-makers, those who wanted to participate in the creation of

something new and different, for the most part immigrated to the United States, not to British North America. The Americans got Thomas Paine; we got Susanna Moodie. Even with the excitement of Confederation, political nationalism here was low-keyed. There were poets, minor and major, who sang the new nation, but always with the bilateral sentiments of Helen Johnson's "Our Native Land", which goes in part:

How many loving memories throng
Round Britain's stormy coast!
Renowned in story and in song,
Her glory is our boast!

With loyal hearts we still abide
Beneath her sheltered wing;
While with true patriot love and pride
To Canada we cling![7]

Well they clung all right, but it was mainly to the "old country". On the French-Canadian side, we find people like Octave Crémazie also clinging, taking inspiration from the glories of a rediscovered France in his *Chant du vieux soldat canadien* or *Le Drapeau de Carillon*. And one could go on and on. Naturally, the fact that each of the two major linguistic groups of Canada derived from an overwhelmingly powerful cultural tradition did not exactly expedite political nationalism in this country. Indeed, to protect itself from the other and the Americans, each major ethnic group constantly reaffirmed its links with its ancestors, and terms like "our martial sires", "founding races", "nos aïeux", and "notre maître, le passé" became the lexicon of nationalism in Canada. With the exception of a few visionaries like Lorne Pierce, political nationalism remained largely the preserve of politicians, and not all politicians at that, for it was the politicians who opened the door to foreign economic control and even permitted for a time the immigration policy of this country to be directed by outsiders. Creative writers have tended more toward critiques and lamentations, such as Douglas Le Pan's "A Country Without a Mythology", Earle Birney's "Canada: A Case History", and numerous works of Gaston Miron, Jacques Brault, Gérald Godin, and other poets of Quebec. But it is not my purpose here to lament the lamentations. On the contrary, considering the negative character and pitfalls of political nationalism, it is possible to reflect that this country has been miraculously blessed in its failure to melt into a single patriotic blob. And of particular interest is what is happening now.

At the moment, we are witnessing several explosions of cultural nationalism — in Quebec, in the Acadian Maritimes, in various parts of English Canada — and the phenomenon certainly invites close attention. What is intriguing about it is that it no longer looks backward for justification and inspiration. The cultural nationalism afoot today is not a determined extension of the past, reaching back over the seas; it is a native product, springing from the actualities of contemporary Canada. Even the famous Frère Untel, who once harangued Quebec on the vital necessity of establishing here the standard French of France, has stated: "We have succeeded in expressing our part of North America in French. There is no reason to deny our accent. And our French has many legitimate expressions. If a Parisian does not understand them, that's his problem." Whereas Frère Untel, whose name incidentally is Jean-Paul Desbiens, at one time characterized Quebec joual as the "absence of language", he now says there is a "profound psychological need" to function in Quebec French. He draws a parallel between the "linguistic bursting-forth" of colloquial-language authors such as Gilles Vigneault and Michel Tremblay and Rabelais's breaking the "barriers of Latin" to write the language of the people of fifteenth-century France.[8]

Axel Maugey, in the introduction to his *Poésie et société au Québec*, states: "La culture québécoise s'en est ressentie. Les diverses expressions cherchent à rompre avec la culture traditionnelle et les valeurs qui la sous-tendaient. . . . Les poètes québécois se chargent de définir l'exacte identité américaine de leur pays." — *Quebec culture is making itself felt. There is a seeking to break with the traditional culture and the values which sustained it. Quebec poets have taken upon themselves to define the exact American identity of their country.* Note the adjective "American", used of course in the broad, continental sense. It should also be noted that Maugey is only echoing what a number of critics and writers have already stated or implied in various ways. In the 1971 issue of the valuable yearly survey of Quebec literature, *Livres et auteurs québécois*, former editor Adrien Thério devotes the opening essay to the subject "La lumière nous viendrait-elle de la France?" In this essay he says: "En gros, ma proposition se résumera un peu à ceci: ce n'est ni sur la France ni sur les Français que les Québécois doivent compter pour savoir si leur littérature est intéressante ou non, c'est sur eux-mêmes uniquement." — *We do not need France or the French to judge our literature; we'll do it by ourselves.* But it is Jacques Godbout who probably expresses the complete rationale involved when he writes in the preface to *Le Couteau sur la table*: "C'est pourquoi ce roman, s'il fait encore partie de la 'littérature française,' est peut-être déjà plus près de celle de francité, dont parle Berque. Dans cette francité nous nous reconnaissons, de Dakar à Montréal; mais plutôt qu'être *Français*, d'une façon personnelle, nous préférons maintenant être *nous-mêmes en français.*" In other words, Godbout is suggesting that the contemporary Quebecker feels part of the widespread francophone world, *la francité.* The former cultural traits of clinging to mother France or of xenophobic isolationism have gone the way of the old "revenge-of-the-cradle" idea. Moreover, les Québécois, rather than thinking of themselves as French, prefer now to *be* themselves, North Americans who speak French. Being themselves unequivocally means being part of contemporary North America, being in *l'améri- canité*, to use the expression which has gained currency .There is, incidentally, no contradiction between *la francité* and *l'américanité*. One can be in both, just as an African, for instance, can be part of *la francité* without in any way compromising his identity as an African.

The phenomenon of *américanité* is not limited, incidentally, to intellectuals. It is something which has seeped upwards rather than filtered down. Yvon Deschamps, the popular and talented Quebec monologuist, who will be discussed at length in another essay in this book, provides an intriguing example. Perhaps his best-known monologue, a veritable linguistic claymore that cuts both ways, is a Québécois worker bragging about how he received an invitation to visit the splendid home of his "bon boss" one Sunday afternoon. No sooner is he there than the boss brings out a lawn mower. The worker is deeply moved by the honour of cutting the grass while his "bon boss" entertains some friends, and he is even more grateful when rewarded with a glass of warm beer. Regarding this monologue and Deschamps' work in general, Professor Laurent Mailhot of l'Université de Montréal has observed in *Canadian Literature*: "Par rapport à la politique, aux mass-média, aux jeunes, à la nouvelle culture, le héros de Deschamps est nous tous, non seulement qué- bécois mais américain, occidental"[9] — *Deschamps' hero is all of us, not only Quebeckers but Americans, Westerners.*

The new cultural nationalism of Quebec is reflected in the quantity, quality, and variety of its literary production, not to mention dynamic activity in other fields such as the visual arts, music, film, and theatre. Here are some startling facts about Quebec television as outlined by Bill Stephenson in the *Canadian Magazine*: "Unlike CBC's English network — which relies heavily on the U.S. for most of its prime-time attractions — French-Canadian TV is mostly home-made. Montreal, producing up to 80 hours per week of original programs, outranks both New York and Los Angeles as separate production centres. Until recently, Montreal turned out more original material than London and Paris combined." Stephenson goes on to point out that "the French network has made at least three filmed series much larger than 'Jalna'." One, "D'Iberville", based on the life of the Montreal-born military genius Pierre Le Moyne, Sieur d'Iberville, has had a huge success in Europe since being first televised in Canada in 1967–68.[10]

There is hardly any need for me to elaborate further. Names like Jutra, Vigneault, Bujold, Charlebois, Julien, Loranger, Barbeau, or Tremblay are known across the country, as well as in Europe and the United States. Established writers are continuing to produce at a bewildering rate — Jacques Ferron, Gérard Bessette, Claude Jasmin, André Langevin, Yves Thériault, Jean-Jules Richard, Anne Hébert, Jacques Godbout — while numerous younger writers are establishing themselves. Indeed, in the 1971 bibliography of Quebec publications, there are some 400 authors listed; the 1974 list has more than 600 names; and the 1976 promises to be in the 800 range. There can be no doubt, then, as to the success of the current upsurge of cultural nationalism in Quebec, despite periodic announcements on the part of leaders of the Montreal St-Jean Baptiste Society, ministers of the Parti Québécois government, and others that the French language is in grave danger, that Quebec culture will soon be reduced to folklore in remote rural areas. Personally, I do not see it. Perhaps there is a problem of definition. If by culture the doomsayers mean the attitudes and lifestyle, the *soupe aux pois*, the twenty-four-children families, *monsieur le curé*, and all that of erstwhile Quebec, then these have already become folklore. But the distinctive attitudes and manners which now set les Québécois apart from other North Americans while at the same time permitting them to adapt to twentieth-century North America, that culture is very much alive.

Whatever their mother tongue, there can be no doubt that more people are speaking French in Quebec today than ever before. The man in the street knows that — the shopping housewife, the car driver, the union member, the theatre-goer. In Sherbrooke, for example, a city of more than 80,000 people, only one remaining movie house shows films in English, and that only on the occasion of a highly-touted release. We have already noted the vigorous activity in the arts. Does all this sound like the swansong of a dying culture? A changing culture, a culture making adjustments to twentieth-century reality and experiencing something of what Alvin Toffler calls "future shock", yes. But by no stretch of the imagination a dying culture. To quote Adrien Thério again, in an issue of *Livres et auteurs québécois* where he answers disparaging remarks by French critics: "En somme, ce Québec malade se porte assez bien."

But Quebec is not alone. The Acadians, the French-speaking people of the Maritimes, have discovered a new cultural nationalism of their own. Like Quebeckers, the Acadians have long depended on real or imagined glories of the past to sustain them, as one can see in Napoléon Landry's well-known collection *Poèmes de mon pays*, published in 1949. Recently, however, a group of writers, most of them quite young — Ronald Després, Antonine Maillet, Léonard Forest, Louis Cormier, and Raymond LeBlanc among them — are reassessing the position of the Acadian in terms of present reality. Antonine Maillet's novel *Pointe aux Coques* is a kind of updated combination of *Maria Chapdelaine* and *Evangeline*, with a heroine quietly choosing the relatively hard life of Acadia over opportunities in the United States. But the reassessment can often be brutal and crude, as illustrated in Maillet's play *La Sagouine* or in this poem by Raymond LeBlanc called "Je suis Acadien":

Je jure en anglais
Tous mes goddam de bâtard
Et souvent les fuck it
Me remontent à la gorge
Avec des Jésus-Christ
Projetés contre le windshield
Saignant Medium Rare
Si au moins j'avais quelques tabernacles
à douze étages
et des hosties toastées
Je saurais que je suis québécois
Et que je sais me moquer
Des cathédrâles de la peur
Je suis acadien
Je me contente d'imiter le parvenu
Avec son Chrysler shiné
Et sa photo dans les journaux
Combien de jours

Me faudra-t-il encore
Avant que ce'te quy icitte
Me run over
Quand je cross la street
Pour me crosser dans la chambre
Et qu'on m'enterre enfin
Dans un cimetière
Comme tous les autres
Au chant de Tu retourneras en poussière
Et puis marde
Qui dit que l'on ne l'est pas déjà
Je suis acadien
Ce qui signifie
Multiplié, fourré,
Dispersé, acheté,
Aliéné, vendu,
Révolté.
Homme déchiré vers l'avenir.[11]

Without doubt there is a special bitterness in Raymond LeBlanc's poetry, a despair and a linguistic violence which seem greater than can be found in the most bitter of current Quebec poetry. Interestingly enough, LeBlanc looks at the Québécois with envy, suggesting the twin realizations that Quebec's current cultural manifestation is not his own and that, compared to his own, it is solid and secure. These attitudes are at least partly justified. In the issue of *Livres et auteurs québécois* for 1971 to which we have already referred, editor Adrien Thério, while discussing Quebec cultural independence, mentions the francophones of New Brunswick: "Il y a peu de Québécois qui sont prêts à aller sauver l'Acadie. . . ." — *Few Quebeckers are ready to go save the Acadians.* The Acadians, then, are largely on their own, unless perhaps more anglophone New Brunswickers and other Canadians become interested enough in the prospects of cultural diversity and enrichment to support the Acadians in their efforts at self-assertion.

On the other hand, far more important than the bitterness in LeBlanc's poetry is the fact that the poetry is there, the fact that something is being written. The work of contemporary Acadian writers is decidedly positive — it reflects a new consciousness, a refusal to remain disciples, a vigorous expression of strengthening cultural nationalism, a new-found dignity. The Acadian, like the Quebecker of a few years ago, is determined to stop being the Canadian counterpart of Ralph Ellison's "invisible man". And that alone is a crucial step forward. It means that there is now for Acadians a possible future as well as a legendary past.

It is of interest to note, incidentally, that the "Cajuns" or Acadians of Louisiana in the United States have embarked upon a cultural renewal of their own, supported by grants from the American federal government no less, and aided by young teachers from France who wish to defer their military service.

But what of cultural nationalism in the English-speaking areas of Canada? Is there anything comparable to the situations in Quebec and New Brunswick? Obviously there is, although the phenomenon is more widespread and varied, therefore more complex. The contemporary English-Canadian author is as conscious as his francophone compatriots of the need to define a cultural identity. He too has broken with the past. To begin with, there has been a great increase in literary production, particularly of books pertaining to Canadian studies. As Robert Fulford states in the introduction to *Read Canadian: A Book About Canadian Books*: "To us it is self-evident . . ." — even the wording here echoes that monumental Declaration of 1776 — "that in Canadian education, Canadian books should play a major role. . . . The editors of *Read Canadian* differ politically in various ways, but we hold in common a point of view that might generally be called nationalist. In cultural terms this means, among other things, that we believe Canadians should be encouraged to pay a great deal more attention to Canada and the Canadian story than they have in the past." And the attention is indeed being paid. New courses are springing forth in high schools and universities across the land. New magazines for creative writing and criticism have appeared from coast to coast. And the older magazines are flourishing — the pioneer review *Canadian Literature*, founded by George Woodcock only a decade and a half ago, used to solicit contributions. Now it receives enough quality material to bring out several extra numbers a year, if finances permitted. And books of Canadian criticism, poetry, fiction, and everything else — it has now become an impossible task to keep up with all of them. Small, independent Canadian publishing houses started the ball rolling, and now even the giant, foreign-owned firms are tagging along. There are, of course, still problems, particularly in the area of editing and distribution of Canadian work, but it is hoped these will be resolved before long.

More important than what is happening on the outside, however, is what is happening inside the minds of English-Canadian writers.

There is a new confidence, an escape from the self-consciousness of the young Hugh MacLennan (who justifiably felt that he had to "map out the territory") in *Barometer Rising* or the careful evasiveness of Stephen Leacock and Morley Callaghan with respect to nationalistic issues. The confidence can be seen in the works of accomplished writers like Margaret Laurence, Robertson Davies, Robert Kroetsch, and Alice Munro in books such as *The Diviners, Fifth Business, Gone Indian,* or *Lives of Girls and Women.* It can also be seen in works of relatively new authors such as Richard Wright, and I am by no means exhausting the list of examples.

Another notable aspect of contemporary writing in English Canada is the use of Africa as a setting in order to examine the complexities of the Canadian character and group psychology. The technique, to be sure, is not new. When Americans were beset with the problems of definition and identity similar to those we have in Canada today, Henry James used European settings in the same way. There is, moreover, a good measure of Jamesian sensitivity and intricacy in David Godfrey's *The New Ancestors* and Hugh Hood's *You Can't Get There from Here,* two of the Canadian novels with African settings, both of which develop into complex allegory pertaining to Canada and Canadians today. A third novel, David Knight's *Farquharson's Physique and What It Did to His Mind,* about the death of a Toronto professor in Nigeria, is a straightforward narrative, but the hero certainly fits into the long tradition of Canadian Calvinistic losers discussed in the previous essay.

This essay, however, is primarily concerned with the larger implications of contemporary nationalism rather than with individual authors and works. As we have seen, evidence abounds to show that in both English and French Canada there is expanding awareness and expression of a new cultural nationalism. The big question is, of course, if different major ethnic groups — Quebeckers, Acadians, and English Canadians — are all seeking their own particular self-realization independent of the others, then how is the centre going to hold? Can the new cultural nationalism not be transformed into fragmented political nationalism, with its customary attributes of xenophobia, prejudice, and narrow self-righteousness, so that things eventually fall apart? I imagine that it can. Already we can see certain danger signals, the blatant anti-Americanism sometimes pursued in English Canada, the anti-English-Canadian sentiments occasionally expressed in French Canada, the fear-mongering everywhere — exploitation of the fear of French takeovers, of English takeovers, of American takeovers, even of Japanese, German, and Amerindian takeovers. But for the time being, the positive qualities of cultural nationalism, the simple desire for self-assertion, group preservation, and dignity are predominant. Moreover, we have already noted that the new nationalism in both French and English Canada contrasts sharply with the inward-turning isolationism and rearview-mirror rationale of such movements in the past. The Quebecker thinks of himself as part of *la francité* and *l'américanité*; the English Canadian is at last seriously aware of Quebec and is also exploring associations with the emerging nations of the Third World. The new cultural nationalism, therefore, has a number of different levels.

Cultural conditioning itself is a process of different levels — a kind of "tabernacle à plusieurs étages", to give the Acadian poet's phrase a new twist. It begins with the immediate family in the home and the adoption of certain basic attitudes and values, then it eases the individual into ever-widening communities — the family outside the home, the village or district, the county, and so forth. Ideally, the process should continue until the individual feels of a piece with all mankind. But generally that doesn't happen, or at least hasn't happened on any significant scale in the past. At some point cultural conditioning seems to stop being a passport and to become a barrier to further integration. At some point cultural nationalism is transformed into political nationalism, and self-realization becomes the imposition of one's attitudes on others. What causes this turning point to be reached? I can suggest two explanations.

The first is that cultural nationalism can reach the level of stagnant self-confidence. If, when that happens, the nation concerned is militarily powerful, and if within its culture and religion (and religion is an all-important factor) the warrior values predominate, then the nation will become self-righteous, arrogant, and obsessed with the duty of imposing its values on peoples it considers unenlightened. The empire-building eras of Greece, Rome, Spain, Portugal, France, and Britain are patent illustrations. Our neighbour to the south, the United States of America, provides another. I can recall former President Lyndon Johnson, in a speech on television, tearfully describing how during his boyhood in Texas there were no streetlights and telephones and electric refrigerators, how effort and skill had eventually provided all these amenities, and how if the Vietnamese would only co-operate, they could have the same. I am sure that it never occurred to Mr. Johnson that the Vietnamese might not want the same. In any event, I am not concerned with the United States. The most astute critics of what may be wrong with the American system are the Americans themselves, and they must solve their own problems. The point I want to make is that the first cause for cultural nationalism converting into political nationalism does not apply to Canada. For one thing, we are nowhere near stagnant cultural self-confidence, and the particular circumstances of Canada with its multilateral nationalism are almost a guarantee that we will never approach such a state. Secondly, we are not militarily powerful, nor will we ever be in the foreseeable future. Thirdly, in reaction to the past and present conditions of the world, warrior values do not predominate in our new cultural nationalism, and religion is no longer the force that it used to be. We may have the Sunday-morning syndrome, occasional hangovers from our Calvinist-Jansenist binges, but we do not have the church militant marching off to war.

The second explanation for cultural nationalism going wrong is the opposite of the first. It is that cultural nationalism, instead of developing to the point of confidence, is thwarted, either from within the ethnic group or from the outside. Herein lies the great danger for Canada. Cultural self-realization cannot be thwarted without the effect of group frustration and demoralization, which in turn lead to degradation and acts of desperation. South African literature — Richard Rive's *Emergency* or Alex La Guma's *A Walk in the Night* — tells us something about that. Both Quebeckers and Acadians have been thwarted for generations, from within and from without. So have various segments of English Canada. As long as we had the mighty opiate of a religion which glorified suffering on earth and education which extolled the heroics of the past, we did not realize that we were hurting. As long as we remained essentially unaware, busy with the everyday tasks of survival, we simply endured. But that is all over. Now we have become hyperconscious, and the cultural nationalism throughout Canada is informed, vigorous, and determined to achieve the goal of self-realization. And it seems to me that there is no good reason why this goal cannot be achieved, and by each Canadian group in its own way. Furthermore, to go back to one of our opening ideas, if rather than a centre this country has a number of different focal points, then we can stop worrying about whether or not the centre will hold.

Canada, after a long stupor, is now awake and poised to become a viable pluralist society, a society where distinct cultural groups co-exist and are held together by a loose, flexible federation. Progress toward viable pluralism in Canada could, of course, be hampered, even arrested. It could be obliterated by the political separation of Quebec. It could be impeded by inflexible federalism, the attempted superimposition of political nationalism. Canada does not need strong, single-minded leaders in the traditional sense; it needs great compromisers. The country was founded on compromise, and without compromise it could become unfounded. The progress toward functional pluralism can also be impeded by the thwarting of cultural nationalism. It is essential that francophone Quebeckers and Acadians continue to develop and to increase their cultural security; it is essential that English-speaking Canadians accept and foster the process. And for English-speaking Canadians, it is essential that they gain control of the machinery for their own cultural and economic development, machinery still often in the hands of foreign investors.

Presuming, then, that Canadian cultural nationalism in its several variations is not thwarted but continues to develop apace, will our society increase in its diversity at the expense of unity? I do not think so. Diversity there will always be, and that is devoutly to be wished, but it must be kept in mind that there are different levels of cultural nationalism. The separate cultural manifestations of contemporary Canada, however much they may differ, have a lot more in common than the game of hockey. They have a whole range of shared experience, attitudes, and values. After all, everybody is in twentieth-century North America. We are all in *l'américanité*. It no longer takes months for people in Vancouver to find out what is going on in Quebec City. And a number of us at least have stopped looking back at our differences. We have stopped being disciples, and the new Canadian hero is emerging throughout the country simultaneously. The new nationalism, in contrast to the old, is a mind-expanding rather than a limiting phenomenon. It is reasonable to suppose that once a measure of cultural security is attained for all, then communication among groups will greatly increase, interawareness will be heightened, and the common values will be acknowledged and come to the fore. Indeed, communication between French and English Canada, ironically given a tremendous boost by the election victory of René Lévesque and his Parti Québécois, is already growing rapidly, as activity in the field of translation attests. We have to a large extent solved the problem of the "invisible man".

What is needed now is even more communication, which will bring about greater inter-group awareness and understanding. In this endeavour, our writers, artists, media people, schools, and universities have a vital role to play, an unfamiliar role perhaps so far as some schools and universities are concerned. It is a role which must emphasize the positive character of pluralistic cultural nationalism and the value of diversity. Outdated concepts of political nationalism, of union based upon domination, conformity, or homogeneity must be set aside. In Canada, our lack of oneness, our respect for disunity is our strength. That is perhaps part of what Frank Scott had in mind when he wrote the following poem called "Union":

Come to me
Not as a river willingly downward falls
To be lost in a wide ocean
But come to me
As flood-tide comes to shore-line
Filling empty bays
With a white stillness
Mating earth and sea.

Union
Exact and complete
Of still separate identities.

3.
War in a Rearview Mirror

The Naked and the Dead, Bridge on the River Kwai, From Here to Eternity, Catch 22 — these are the novels which I suppose, with a little prodding from the movie industry, are most likely to come to mind when one thinks about literature and the Second World War. No Canadian author has ever achieved notable fame as a war novelist; yet Canada has in fact produced a number of excellent war novels in both English and French. It is fitting, therefore, to depart briefly from our discussion of contemporary trends in Canadian literature and have a look at war in the Canadian novelists' rearview mirror.

The effects of war are recorded in different ways. Part of the story is told by statistics: the number of dead and wounded in a battle, the amount of property destroyed, the ships sunk, the planes shot down, the tonnage of bombs dropped — figures can stagger the imagination. The larger statistics — 6,000,000 Jews exterminated, 24,133 ships lost at sea, 15,300,000 soldiers killed and wounded, 42,022 Canadian servicemen lost on active service — these can stun the mind to the point of incomprehension. The larger the number, the vaguer it must be and the more removed from understandable reality. And that is where the writers come in.

The function of a good war writer is to bring us back to the grim reality in terms which we can grasp, in ways that we can feel. Instead of strategy and numbers, he examines the effects of war on the individual, on the human being who, willingly or unwillingly, has been drawn into one of the most intense and traumatic experiences possible in life. And the writer's function takes on added importance today, considering that in general two generations of Canadians have not known that experience.

The Canadian writers who performed the function, performed it well. Among them is Lionel Shapiro, who wrote three books: *The Sealed Verdict, Torch for a Dark Journey*, and *The Sixth of June*. Hugh Garner described six days on a Canadian corvette in *Storm Below*. Ralph Allen probed the whole question of propaganda and truth in his *Homemade Banners* and *The High White Forest,* and Norman Levine's *The Angled Road* is about an airman trying to understand himself. In his comic novel *Turvey,* Earle Birney looked at the funny side of war, but did not escape the tragic. Jean-Jules Richard's *Neuf jours de haine* deals with the bitter transformation war can produce on the personality, while William Allister's *A Handful of Rice* is a shattering and unflattering account of Canadians in a Japanese prisoner-of-war camp in Malaya, an experience which the author and a few others captured at Hong Kong somehow managed to live through.

Perhaps the best of Canadian war novels, in fact ranking with the best of all war novels, are Colin McDougall's *Execution* and Jean Vaillancourt's *Les Canadiens errants.* In these books the whole spectrum of emotions caused by war is dramatically presented.

The effects of the pressure of war and killing, of course, vary from individual to individual, and these variations are duly and often sensitively registered in the war novels. At the same time, reading these books one sees that there are certain common patterns of behaviour. The first common effect, for instance, is excitement, exhilaration. It would appear that war can appeal to man's desire for adventure and romance. Here is Colin McDougall, in *Execution,* describing the reaction of a Canadian soldier landing in Sicily:

> Weapons cradled in their arms, Lieutenant Adam and his force moved steadily through the parkland. Their steps were cushioned on pine needles. It was quiet in this forest world; noise from outside, like the far-off clatter of machine-gun fire, sounded muffled and remote. Birds sang from the branches overhead.
>
> Adam's step was sure and alert. His whole being was concentrated on the purpose ahead, but today his mind was so brilliantly quick and alive that not even this hugely important first attack was sufficient to contain it. His mind clamoured with the wonder and excitement of all that had happened since the assault landing last night. . . . John Adam thought of himself as a solid, practical person, not given to fanciful flights, but he found mad grandeur in the concept that cities would be made funeral pyres to accomplish the invaders' purpose. This was a night when irresistibly wild poetry rode at sea. (p. 13)

It is probably true that a lot of young Canadians entered the war innocently, convinced that they were on God's side and that He was on theirs. Thus they could find "mad grandeur" in watching a city burn, even though they understood that people were burning too.

Like the bombardier who presses a button to release tons of explosives, they were at a comfortable distance. *Execution* goes on to describe a padre's reaction to the first events of battle:

> But next he saw John Adam, his friend, standing with his captured charger, surrounded by his victory-flushed men, and admiration swelled inside him to the exclusion of everything else. The affair became something exhilarating. . . . They were all here on God's errand, and they were doing men's work. These were exciting times, and he was glad to be living them. (p. 30)

Unfortunately, the gladness, the romance, the initial excitement and exhilaration of war do not last long. They soon give way to realization of the seriousness of affairs, of the fact that war is not a game but a matter of life and death, and of life constantly in the face of death. In *The Sixth of June*, Lionel Shapiro captures the essence of this sobering realization:

> It was as though the light breeze weaving in off the Channel had been whispering ominously. The atmosphere on the docks was heavy with foreboding.
>
> Medical officers, nursing sisters, and orderlies stood about in small silent groups in the warming sun outside the three huge tents of the casualty clearing station which had been set up during the night. Senior officers, some with red tabs on their lapels and wearing handsome glengarries, peered out to sea from the edge of the landing stage. The townfolk were lined along the sea wall, their faces scrubbed and solemn as on a churchgoing day. Even the children frolicking in the streets behind the sea wall seemed to understand they must not laugh or shout. . . .
>
> A Canadian brigadier, tall and slim and crisply handsome, shaded his eyes as he looked out to sea. "The battle is still engaged," he said curtly, "heavily engaged." He walked a piece down the landing stage in a clear manoeuvre to avoid further inquiry. . . . Two jeep-loads of war correspondents and photographers roared in, looked about, and roared away, but not before they had left a rumor in their wake that the first news would soon break on the wireless. By the time it came, almost everyone in the dock area had converged on the signals shed.
>
> "The Prime Minister has just informed the House of Commons," an immaculate bbc voice announced, "that shortly before dawn this morning a strong Canadian force, joined by small elements of British troops and escorted by ships of the Royal Navy, drove onto the French coast in the vicinity of Dieppe." (pp. 120–21)

Dieppe, a small coastal town on the Channel which had hitherto meant nothing to the average Canadian — the name still rings with tragedy and bitterness. Who was responsible for the senseless slaughter? Why were young men from across the nation sent to make their way up open beaches against machine-gun fire from concrete pillboxes? Were those in command still brilliant to the tops of their boots, as Churchill is said to have remarked of General Douglas Haig in the First World War? Is it true that rawboned Canadian troops, restless, bored, and eager for action, were terrorizing the English communities where their training camps were located, and that Churchill himself decided to teach them a lesson? If so, some lesson!

But whatever the case, after the exhilaration, then the realization of seriousness, it is only a matter of time until the war produces the effect of crushing disillusionment. The traditional values, the hallowed notions of courage, goodness, justice, decency, and mercy are shattered as flesh and bones are shattered indiscriminately by exploding shells. Now the predominant factor is the basic urge to survive. The war novels illustrate that men confronted with brutality are invariably reduced to performing the same kind of brutality. War can cause a man to discover the bestiality within himself, something which may have remained hidden under the normal circumstances of a reasonably tranquil and conventional life, the office, the commuter train, the Christmas party. In McDougall's *Execution*, the brutality begins when Canadian soldiers, on orders from headquarters, must shoot two innocent and confused Italians who have been more or less adopted as mascots of the unit. When a German prisoner spits in the face of Lanthier, one of the characters in Vaillancourt's novel *Les Canadiens errants*, he reacts as follows:

> "Ah, mon enfant-de-chienne!" he hissed. He had grabbed his Sten by the strap, breaking a branch off a tree as he swung it through the air. He smashed it into the face of his insulter, knocking him to the ground. Lanthier pointed the barrel at the man's chest and pressed the trigger until the clip was empty. The German's body quivered, then for a few moments went through a hideous convulsion, twisting like a worm. Finally it lay still.[12]

Once he has been reduced to brutality, a man can lose all faith in himself and in the human race. He can become a killing machine, like many of the characters described in Canadian war novels. The way back to the human race then becomes extremely difficult, impossible for some. A temporary solution to the problem is simply to become an automaton following orders, asking no questions, and seeking no understanding of the meaning of it all. In fact, life itself must be treated as meaningless. At this stage, even the desire to live can flicker out. William Allister, in his *A Handful of Rice*, provides a precise illustration:

> The column of struggling prisoners halted. They were divided in groups. Along with a dozen others, Tony was herded against a wall. A machine-gun was placed before them and, in sign language, they were motioned to say their prayers. Tony's dulled brain accepted the act as normal. They would be shot. They would be changed from the living to the dead. It would be right and good. His pain would end. His thirst, his fatigue, his fear of death, his questions, all the horror, would end. He would rest.
>
> Someone was praying in French beside him, loudly, without inhibition, a chant whose rhythm was broken by harsh barking sobs. Some wept softly in animal pain. Others merely gazed before them with relaxed, mindless patience. Tony's hysteria, his nausea, were long past.
>
> He was too tired, too tired to think. He could hardly remember his name or how he came to be here. Just end it, end it, was his only pale desire. (p. 7)

Like Dostoevski, William Allister knew — he had seen the pale horse with the pale rider. At the lowest ebb, then, life is stripped of its meaning and is not worth hanging on to. All the old values, the values learned at home, at school, and in church, in a faraway and long-ago Canada, do not make sense any more, except to provide something to do while waiting to be shot. In a brilliant and moving episode, Colin McDougall dramatizes the depth of nothingness a man can reach, and how some, the lucky ones, can find their way back up. John Adam, McDougall's protagonist, picks up a young Italian girl who is keeping her family from starvation by the only means possible — prostitution:

> He had her in her own bedroom that afternoon, in half darkness with the shutters closed, while her parents and brothers sat gravely in other rooms of the apartment. . . . There had even been a formal offer of wine; and that — for a blazing moment — sent Adam blindly, furiously mad with anger. . . . The daughter of the house represented the family's capital: they sent her out to earn the food they must eat. . . . But Adam's anger cooled. What the hell, he thought: much worse things than this

happen in wartime. . . . He declined the offer of wine and followed
Elena into her room. . . . She spoke more English than he did Italian,
but now:

"Ti amo," Elena said. "I love you."

Adam ignored this. Unresisted, his hand voyaged up and down her
trembling body.

"Say it," she said, half moaning, half tearful. "Say Io ti amo."

"Go to hell," said Adam, going on with what he was doing. He felt her
sobbing under his hands. Then Adam looked into her eyes; he saw the
magnitude of her shame, and suddenly he understood. . . . She wanted
to pretend that he was the man who might, under other, better circumstances, have been her lover. . . .

"Elena," he said. He spoke softly; it was the first time he had used her
name. "Elena. All right. All right then — Io ti amo." . . .

It was pretence, but he had given her something; and, oddly, he felt
better at once, as though he had also given something to himself.
(pp. 89–91)

McDougall's character John Adam learns that even at its worst,
under conditions of war which deprave and degrade human beings,
life can still be bearable if one retains a thread of compassion for
others and a trace of human dignity. In a war the individual can be
reduced to the lowest level of existence, but from within he finds
the power to lift himself up again.

Then comes the final stage of the war's effect on people — readjustment to ordinary civilian life when the fighting is all over.
Some soldiers, as can be seen in Vaillancourt's *Les Canadiens errants*,
will never be able to readjust. They have seen too much. They have
been psychologically crippled. Others have been crippled in different
ways, as Earle Birney's *Turvey*, in a passage which slips from
comedy to tragedy, poignantly illustrates:

Nor does the bombardier at the far end smile when he is lifted into
a stretcher and carried out to the town of his mother and his wife. And
this is rather unsporting of him, for he could laugh, and at least he
might say goodbye to all his mates. The doctors have said that he could
be walking about and enjoying life if he would only snap out of himself,
and they are hoping a few weeks of psychiatric care in a hospital near
home will make him right, or almost right. For the only things missing
about the bombardier are his testicles. (pp. 276–77)

But despite the ravages of war life must go on. When the war has
ended, the fortunate ones come home, never to be quite the same

perhaps, but having no choice but to carry on as best they can. To begin with at least, there is the pleasant feeling of relief, the joy of reunion, the parade of victory. Hugh MacLennan, in his novel *Two Solitudes*, tells about the homecoming:

> They were returning to what they thought was good because it had been familiar. When their ships drew in to Halifax, they smelled their country before it rose to them over the horizon, and their nostrils dilated to the odour of balsam blown out to sea from the evergreen forests that cover most of Nova Scotia like a shaggy hide. . . . They paraded through the city, and on the reviewing stand on Sherbrooke Street generals with red tabs and red officer-faces and politicians with grey faces and silk hats saluted them. . . . They marched through Montreal, and the pipers played them along with *The Blue Bonnets* and *The Hundred Pipers*, and before the French-Canadian regiment the band played *Sambre et Meuse*.
>
> The women were the ones you noticed in the crowd, for the day was more theirs than the troops'. You could see the tight, grey faces of the ones whose men were not there, and you could also see an unusually naked expression in the others. These strained for the sight of a single man, eyes leaping to the familiar face when it marched into view while in a private agony each woman hoped to find it the same, still lovable, able to be magnetized back to the cage again from what it had seen and where it had been, from the horror and the hunting and the Champs Elysées and Regent Street, to the suburban house and the tenement, the groceries, doctor's bills, insurance premiums, pay cheques, slippers before the fire and three square meals a day. (p. 182)

Hugh MacLennan thus brings us back to the gladness, completing the circle. And together, as I have tried to let the books themselves illustrate, Canadian war novels cover all the segments of the circle. They provide a total and powerful impression of war — its thrills, its horrors, its glory, its boredom, its madness, and ironically, its momentary periods of profound peace.

4.
Thoughts on Five Writers

There is no special reason why I should have chosen the five writers to be discussed in the next few pages rather than five others, except that either some aspect of the author's work in general or a particular book has caught and held my attention. With regard to Frederick Philip Grove, I find the mysterious phenomenon of the man and his complete works quite intriguing. André Langevin's latest novel, *Une Chaîne dans le parc*, has already been examined in the first essay in this volume, but his earlier novel *Poussière sur la ville* is still my favourite. Likewise, Gérard Bessette's *La Bagarre* is to my mind one of the important landmarks of Quebec literature. The significance of the monologue tradition and of its leading exponent in Quebec today, Yvon Deschamps, certainly warrants attention. And finally, what more appropriate book for fifth position than Robertson Davies' *Fifth Business*.

WHAT WAS FREDERICK PHILIP GROVE?

In recent years, any discussion of Frederick Philip Grove has been dominated by two questions. The first question, and a basic one at that, is: *who* was he? And the second question, of course, is: *what* was he?

After many months of detective work by Professor Douglas Spettigue and others, the question of Grove's true identity appears to be reaching a satisfactory resolution. There is still, however, considerable confusion as to exactly what kind of writer he was. The frantic search for Grove the man has left something of a mess in the area of critical analysis of his works, and the time has come to tidy up, to put things in their proper places. Grove has been called a realist, a naturalist, a romanticist, and on the basis of what he passed off as his official autobiography, a calculating fantasist, or at least a man given to embroidery of the truth. Sometimes Grove is categorized as a realist writing in a naturalistic manner, sometimes as a naturalist writing realistic fiction, sometimes as a tragedian who embraces romanticism. And to complicate the situation further, judging from Grove's own essays and critical writings, one eventually realizes that Frederick Philip Grove had his own peculiar notions of the meanings of all these literary terms, notions often quite divorced from the definitions now generally accepted. If Grove could come back from the dead — presuming, of course, that he is dead; I for one am now leery of taking anything about Frederick Philip Felix Paul Greve Grove for granted — if he could come back, then he would be able to save the Canada Council a lot of money and Canadian scholars a lot of effort by clearing up the remaining mysteries about exactly who he was. But considering the foggy nature of his grasp of literary terminology, even he himself would not be able to tell us precisely what he was. That we must decide for ourselves.

The problem, it seems to me, lies in the understanding of what realism, naturalism, and romanticism mean with respect to fiction writing. Can an author be more than one at the same time? Was Grove both naturalist and realist? Because if he was not, then a good many critics have been barking up the wrong tree. Accordingly, as a precautionary measure, I propose to begin this study by exploring the precise meanings of the terms realism, naturalism, and romanticism, then to apply the conclusions to Grove's writings, both critical essays and fiction.

Romanticism as it applies to novel writing is perhaps the simplest starting point. We are all familiar with the various aspects of the Romantic Movement in literature, and we know that among leading critics and authors there were many and varying interpretations of these aspects. "Yet," as Thrall, Hibbard, and Holman point out in their standard reference text called *A Handbook to Literature*:

> . . . viewed in philosophical terms, *romanticism* does have a fairly definite meaning for the student of literature. The term designates a literary and philosophical theory which tends to see the individual at the very center of all life and all experience, and it places him, therefore, at the center of art, making literature most valuable as an expression of his unique feelings and particular attitudes. . . . Employing the commonplace, the natural, the simple as materials, it seeks always to find the Absolute, the Ideal, by transcending the actual; whereas realism finds its values in the actual, and naturalism in the scientific laws which undergird the actual. (pp. 231–32)

In their book entitled *Realism and Romanticism in Fiction*, Current-Garcia and Patrick make the following additional distinction. Romanticists, they observe, are characterized by "their insistence upon the artist's obligation to create in his fiction an imaginary world which, however closely it might resemble the world of actual fact, would nevertheless idealize character and action in order to stress the desirable ends of human life" (p. 6). In other words, the romanticist begins with an ideal, a message, or a point of some sort, and he shapes his materials to prove that point. He thinks of himself as the centre of all life, and he seeks to find an absolute or an ideal by transcending the actual. His work, then, is synthesis rather than analysis; he manipulates his subject matter to suit his end, rather than allowing the end to be determined by the nature of the subject matter.

Now on the basis of these observations it is clear that Frederick Philip Grove was not a romanticist. Indeed, he would have shuddered at the suggestion. Grove himself equated romanticism with inferiority. Comparing Flaubert and Zola, he states in "Realism in Literature", one of the essays in his book *It Needs to Be Said*: "Of the two, Flaubert was a realist — that is to say, first of all an artist; Zola, because his aim lay outside of the domain of art, was a romantic" (p. 58). With regard to Shakespeare and Marlowe, in the same essay Grove claims that the former was a realist while the latter, Marlowe, was a romantic. In Marlowe's case, however, he is labeled a romantic not because "his aim lay outside of the domain of art" but because the reader is "instantly aware of his personal predilections".

But we need not linger over the vagaries and inconsistencies of Grove's own attempts at definition. He himself admits: "It is clear, of course, that this definition, no matter what its value may be, labors from the outset under the immense disadvantage of ignoring the critical thought of almost all that have gone before" (p. 50). I am not sure that being able to ignore all those who have gone before is necessarily a disadvantage, but it certainly lets Grove off the hook. What is more important, however, is his statement that "what makes a work of literature or any other craft a work of art is the fact that it mirrors a more or less universal human reaction to what is not I" (p. 62). He was concerned with what he calls the universal "reaction of the human soul to the fundamental condition of man's life on earth," and his works, even something so close to his personal experience as *Over Prairie Trails*, faithfully reflect that concern. The basic romanticist principle of literature as the expression of the author's "unique feelings and particular attitudes", Grove rejected completely. Unlike that of the romanticists, his work is analysis rather than synthesis, although it should be noted that he shared with the romanticists the belief that a writer must transcend the actual, the surface detail of life. But he insisted on presenting life as he saw it rather than shaping materials to an end, and he did not seek the ideal or the absolute.

But whether or not Grove was a romanticist has never really been an issue of importance. The relationship of his attitudes and his works to naturalism and realism is where the true problem lies. And once again it is expedient to turn to Thrall, Hibbard, and Holman's *Handbook to Literature*. They define realism as follows:

> Realism is, in the broadest sense, simply fidelity to actuality in its representation in literature. . . . In order to give a more precise definition, however, one needs to limit it to the movement which arose in the nineteenth century, at least partially in reaction against romanticism, which was centered on the novel, and which was dominant in France, England, and America from roughly mid-century to the closing decade, when it was replaced by naturalism. . . .
>
> Generally, the realist is a believer in pragmatism, and the truth he seeks to find and express is a relativistic truth, associated with discernible consequences and verifiable by experience. Generally, too, the realist is a believer in democracy, and the materials he elects to describe are the common, the average, the everyday. Furthermore, *realism* can be thought of as the ultimate of middle-class art, and it finds its subjects in bourgeois life and manners. Where the romanticist transcends the immediate to find the ideal, and the naturalist plumbs the actual to find the scientific laws which control its actions, the realist centers his attention to a remarkable degree on the immediate, the here and now, the specific action, and the verifiable consequence. . . .
>
> The surface details, the common actions, and the minor catastrophes of a middle-class society constituted the chief subject matter of the movement. Most of the realists avoided situations with tragic or cataclysmic implications. Their tone was often comic, frequently satiric, seldom grim or somber. (pp. 397–98)

Considering this definition of realism, the plot already begins to thicken. Grove certainly opted for verisimilitude, however secondary he claims it to be (see *It Needs to Be Said*, p. 70), and he accepted the principle of a "relativistic truth". In fact, in his essay called "The

Happy Ending", he elaborates on the many aspects of truth, noting three in particular — concrete, abstract, and subjective — and reserving the "subjective or emotional truth" for the domain of art. On the other hand, Grove's work can hardly be thought of as "the ultimate of middle-class art", finding "its subjects in bourgeois life and manners". Nor did he avoid, needless to say, "situations with tragic or cataclysmic implications". He was, in fact, obsessed with the idea of tragedy, claiming that only tragedy could be a universal and great work of art.

But let us probe further into the definitions. Here is what Thrall, Hibbard, and Holman say about naturalism:

> In its simplest sense naturalism is the application of the principles of scientific determination to fiction. . . . The fundamental view of man which the naturalist takes is of an animal in the natural world, responding to environmental forces and internal stresses and drives, over none of which he has either control or full knowledge. It tends to differ from realism, not in its attempt to be accurate in the portrayal of its materials but in the selection and organization of those materials, selecting not the commonplace but the representative. . . .
>
> Naturalism is the novelist's response to the revolution in thought that modern science has produced. From Newton it gains a sense of mechanistic determinism; from Darwin (the greatest single force operative upon it) it gains a sense of biological determinism and the inclusive metaphor of the lawless jungle which it has used perhaps more often than any other; from Marx it gains a view of history as a battleground of vast economic and social forces; from Freud it gains a view of the determination of the inner and subconscious self; from Taine it gains a view of literature as a product of deterministic forces; from Comte it gains a view of social and environmental determinism. . . .
>
> American novelists have been generally more receptive to its theories than the English have . . . Frank Norris . . . Stephen Crane . . . Jack London wrote naturalistic novels with Nietzschean "supermen" (and "superdogs") as protagonists.
>
> The novels produced in this school have tended to emphasize either a biological determinism, with an emphasis on the animal nature of man, particularly his heredity, portraying him as an animal engaged in the endless and brutal struggle for survival; or a socio-economic determinism, portraying man as the victim of environmental forces and the product of social and economic factors beyond his control or his full understanding. Occasionally, as in the novels of Thomas Hardy, man is seen as the victim of "destiny" or "fate." But whichever of these views is taken, the naturalist strives to be objective, even documentary, in his

presentation of material. . . . Life, he seems to feel, is a vicious trap, a cruel game. . . . (pp. 301–04)

Now the definition I have just cited is, so far as I can determine from considerable research into the subject, essentially complete and accurate. However, Donald Pizer, in his study called *Realism and Naturalism in Nineteenth-Century American Literature*, offers an additional distinction which is highly apropos so far as the works of Frederick Philip Grove are concerned. He points out that:

> The naturalist populates his novel primarily from the lower middle class or the lower class. . . . His fictional world is that of the commonplace and unheroic in which life would seem to be chiefly the dull round of daily existence, as we ourselves usually conceive of our lives. But the naturalist discovers in this world those qualities of man usually associated with the heroic or adventurous, such as acts of violence and passion which involve sexual adventure or bodily strength and which culminate in desperate moments and violent death. . . .
>   The naturalist often describes his characters as though they are conditioned and controlled by environment, heredity, instinct, or chance. But he also suggests a compensating humanistic value in his characters or their fates which affirms the significance of the individual and of his life. . . . The naturalist appears to say that although the individual may be a cipher in a world made amoral by man's lack of responsibility for his fate, the imagination refuses to accept this formula as the total meaning of life and so seeks a new basis for man's sense of his own dignity and importance. (pp. 12–13)

Donald Pizer's comments, it will be immediately appreciated, apply with almost uncanny appropriateness to the protagonists of Frederick Grove's three novels of the soil, *Our Daily Bread*, *Fruits of the Earth*, and *Two Generations*, to Niels Lindstedt in *Settlers of the Marsh*, and to Len Sterner in *The Yoke of Life*. But in addition to Pizer's there are other subtle distinctions relevant to Grove and his fiction. Malcolm Cowley, for example, in his classic essay called "A Natural History of American Naturalism", mentions that the naturalists tried to achieve the romantic quality of "bigness in its double reference to size and intensity". No "teacup tragedies", to use Frank Norris's phrase. Cowley substantiates his argument by reference to Norris, Dreiser, to Upton Sinclair's *The Jungle*, which deals with the meat-packing industry, and to the various other books on industries which Sinclair and his contemporaries wrote. He could easily have included, we might note here, a Canadian book called *The Master of the Mill.*

Cowley makes another observation worthy of note. Speaking generally of naturalists, he says, "Their objective point of view toward their material was sometimes a pretense that deceived themselves before it deceived others. From the outside world they chose the subjects that mirrored their own conflicts and obsessions" (p. 380). Then Cowley adds an intriguing little remark: "It is their feeling of fascinated revulsion toward their subject matter that makes some of the naturalists hard to read; they seem to be flogging themselves and their audience like a band of penitents" (p. 381). One almost wonders if Malcolm Cowley could have been thinking of Frederick Grove's *Master of the Mill.*

Be that as it may, taking all the above observations into account, what then are the characteristics which differentiate naturalism from realism? They may be summarized as follows:

1. While both realists and naturalists stress fidelity to the details of more or less contemporary life, the realist sees his characters as manipulating their circumstances, whether biological, socio-economic, environmental, or psychological.
2. While both realists and naturalists deal with the actual, the surface details of life, the naturalist does not do so as an end in itself but in order to seek an underlying and universal law or truth.
3. While realists tend to select the commonplace, naturalists lean toward the representative or typical.
4. While realists tend toward a comic or satiric tone, naturalists favour the tragic or cataclysmic implications of the human condition.
5. Naturalists are given to imbuing protagonists, however proletarian in station, with Nietzschean "superman" attributes, creating a heroic struggle between man and his fate, with the latter, to be sure, always emerging the winner. Yet a compensating humanistic value is suggested, affirming the significance of the individual and his life.

Now let us examine Frederick Philip Grove's attitudes and fiction in the light of these five criteria.

1. Grove states in his alleged autobiography, *In Search of Myself,* that "It was an axiom with me that human evolution has not yet freed itself from its animal trammels" (p. 359). In other words,

naturalist principle of the tragic implications of the human condition, and all of his works, including the fantasy *Consider Her Ways*, stand as dramatizations of that principle. His conviction of the "indomitable spirit of mankind" explains the heroic dimensions he gave to man's struggle against fate and the "compensating humanistic value" suggested in all of his novels, causing them to accord precisely with the distinctive features of Donald Pizer's observations on literary naturalism. And as we have already noted, they also accord with the particular distinctions outlined by Malcolm Cowley.

Accordingly, there is no need for doubt or confusion as to the mode of Frederick Philip Grove's fiction. It is clear that if we accept the criteria outlined above, and I believe that we must if we have any regard for the consensus of serious and expert literary scholarship, then we must accept that Frederick Philip Grove was every inch a literary naturalist. Those who have called him a realist or whatever, including Grove himself and several of his leading critics, are simply guilty of inaccuracy or inattention. The evidence is there for all to see. Grove, it should be noted, again because he either did not know or did not care to find out the exact meanings the terms had come to have in literary criticism, insisted on many occasions that he was a realist and not a naturalist. And this insistence may account for the fact that critics were misled.

But what else was Frederick Philip Grove besides a literary naturalist? Before concluding this explanation, I should like to consider certain other aspects of the man's mind.

In many respects, Grove's thought was ahead of his time. I have remarked elsewhere how his novel *The Master of the Mill* deals with problems of labour relations and the effects of automation which are only now beginning to be generally debated in Canada, problems which will be with us for a long time to come and which could well destroy society as we know it today. With regard to the future of Canada and Canadian nationalism, Grove's ideas were also prophetic. He saw Canada as a pluralistic nation, relying upon its pluralism as a bulwark against the domination of the United States of America. Actually, at a time when the fashion was to trumpet Canada's good fortune in sharing the continent with a friendly and powerful nation so similar and closely related in so many ways, Frederick Grove saw the United States as the greatest threat to Canadian cultural and spiritual independence. In his essay on "Nationhood", he states his views as follows:

South of our border lives a mighty nation which is reaching out with its tentacles over the globe — with a view towards the Americanisation, as it is commonly called, of that globe: a nation which, by the help of two processes, has evolved a mechanical civilization unique in the modern world — the two processes being mass-production and standardization (mass-production doing away with artistic aspirations, and standardization with individuality): a nation proud of its wealth and power and proud of its great material civilization. Yet the fact is that all over the world, even in the Latin republics of the western continents, we find today a certain disquietude at the growth of its influence. All over the world, that influence is, by thoughtful minds, considered as dangerous: as a shallowing of ancient standards, as a re-orientation of men's minds and desires, from things spiritual, towards things material and economic. (p. 142)

Grove was certainly right about the "things material and economic" and about the growing sinister influence of the United States. If anything, he underestimated the strength of American influence and overestimated the strength of Canadian resistance. What he did not foresee, perhaps because he, like a number of Canadians today, was blindly anti-American in many respects (he absurdly maintained, for instance, that there was nothing of value in American literature since the transcendentalists), was that American intellectuals would become the severest critics of the United States. But Grove did see clearly how the exploitation of natural resources would become a major issue in Canadian-American relations. And he also realized that the issue was two-sided, involving a combination of Canadian cupidity and American acquisitiveness, a combination of "sell-out" and "take-over". Here is how he puts it:

Great, in dim antiquity, seemed the resources of Spain to the ancient Romans. There is a tradition that the same Romans coveted Britain because its soil held tin. No doubt many of those barbarous Britons grew rich through the trade. In fact, we read in Tacitus that, with the Roman trade, such "alluring vices" — his word for luxuries — "such alluring vices as the porch in front of the house, the bath with hot and cold water, and the pride and pomp of the formal dinner-table" found their way into the remotely northern province. But the canny old philosopher adds, "This sort of thing they, in their ignorance, called culture whereas it was merely part of their slavery." (pp. 135–36)

We have not, as Grove implies, made a great deal of progress. But in general Grove is optimistic about Canada's future, believing that if the principle of true federation, that is to say the union of still distinct and separate cultural identities, each preserving the essential values of its past and respecting the right of others to do likewise, is upheld, then the Canadian nation has unique possibilities in the modern world.

Materialism, to be sure, was one thing which Frederick Philip Grove feared and hated, although his attitude toward material progress did seem to mellow as he grew older. He came to see that for the masses of men a certain amount of physical comfort and security was desirable, and that for the artist to realize his potentialities, it was a necessity. In his old age, Grove would have approved of Canada Council grants. "In the total balance," he says in his autobiography, "the material victories of mankind may, in terms of human happiness, be worth more than the benefits conferred on it by its religious leaders, philosophers, poets, sculptors, painters and musicians combined, though I doubt it" (p. 206). The doubt notwithstanding, that Frederick Grove should allow the possibility of benefit accruing from material progress indicates that he was not as single-minded as is commonly supposed. In fact, I see Grove as a highly complex and profound thinker, and I believe that we are just beginning to appreciate the complexity and depth of his thought. His philosophy seems to lean toward the principle of material progress as a benefit for all of mankind, so long as it is not an end in itself. He believed that every human being was responsible for all other human beings, and like the old Icelander in *The Turn of the Year*, each person should be willing to produce for the sole purpose of bettering the lot of people in general. "Mankind as such," he says in an essay, "must be considered as a unit embarked upon the expedition of life; and mankind includes every Siberian, every Indian, every Chinese who may starve in a famine. Until we have acquired that universal outlook, there can be no true civilization on earth" (pp. 193–94).

Frederick Philip Grove, then, was a feeling humanist as well as a strong Canadian nationalist and a literary naturalist. And undoubtedly he was a good deal besides. The more we find out about who and what this remarkable man was, the more we realize that there is more to know. He seemed to take great delight in challenges in his life. He seemed to prefer to do things the hard way. It is therefore fitting that his own career — his life, his works, his ideas — now stands as a challenge to Canadian literary scholarship.

LANGEVIN AND BESSETTE—
LITERARY HEAVYWEIGHTS OF QUEBEC

Two of the undisputed heavyweights of Quebec letters over the last quarter-century or so are André Langevin and Gérard Bessette. Born in the 1920s, both men began to publish in the 1950s and have continued without a let-up, each following his own distinctive career. Both men are widely read, and one of the few things they have in common is a sensitivity to the trends of contemporary French literature. At the same time, Langevin and Bessette are almost archetypical Québécois writers, and they have been deeply involved in the modern evolution of the literature of French Canada.

Probably *Poussière sur la ville* is still the best known of André Langevin's works. It is the story of a newly married young couple and a company town. And although the marital problems of the couple, a doctor and his adulterous wife, appear at first sight to be the author's predominant concern, the mining town of Thetford Mines (called Macklin in the book) functions at once as locale and major character in the novel. The town surrounds the couple both horizontally and vertically, the reader being aware of the latter through repeated references to asbestos dust in the air and to the miners, on round-the-clock shifts, constantly burrowing underground.

Thetford Mines in recent years, quite apart from the novel and certainly without Langevin's realization at the time of his writing *Poussière sur la ville*, has in an intriguing way collectively paralleled the theme of the book. Along with another Quebec company town in the Eastern Townships, Asbestos, it accounts for a large proportion of the world's asbestos production. The huge mines, foreign-owned to be sure, have created steady employment and relatively good salaries for the depressed region of the Townships; they are also responsible for ecological blight and terrible lung disease (asbestosis) caused by inhaling minute fibers — being a doctor, Langevin's hero Alain Dubois would normally have had excellent prospects for professional success. From the general point of view of Quebec's economy, however, even the employment benefits of the mining operation have lately been seriously questioned, particularly in the light of the fact that the highest paid jobs connected with asbestos (everything apart from digging it out of the ground, that is) are mainly performed in the United States. And the manufactured products, the shingles and sheathing and whatever, cost more to buy in Thetford Mines than in Boston or New York. After all, there is a great deal of costly shipping involved.

Back in 1949, Asbestos and Thetford Mines were the stage for one of the most vicious and bitter labour disputes ever to take place in Quebec. Before it ended clergymen from parish priest to Archbishop Charbonneau as well as provincial Premier Maurice Duplessis were deeply involved, and provincial police were arresting strikers in the sanctuary of confessional booths. But when reporters went back to the mining towns a couple of years ago to check on the current attitude of the workers, they were rudely rebuffed and told to mind their own business. We've got steady jobs, fringe benefits, pensions coming up, so leave us alone, the local people said. They were unmoved by reminders of respiratory ailments, dehumanizing conditions, economic exploitation. In other words, they were exactly like André Langevin's hero Alain Dubois, a race apart, keepers of their own manhood, masochistically determined to see things through to an end, whatever it might be.

Not counting Pierrot in *Une Chaîne dans le parc*, which was discussed earlier, Dubois is a typical Langevin protagonist. Actually there are a number of typical elements found in all four of André Langevin's novels previous to *Une Chaîne* — *Évadé de la nuit*, published in 1951, *Poussière sur la ville*, 1953, *Le Temps des hommes*, 1956, and *L'Élan d'Amérique* (The Moose), which appeared in 1972 — the first two and the last of which, incidentally, were awarded literary prizes. Each of Langevin's first four novels deals with problems of alienation, between parent and child or between husband and wife. In *L'Élan d'Amérique*, he manages to combine both possibilities when the heroine, Claire Peabody, through a complicated series of events winds up married to her father. Each of the novels has orphans, suicides, alcoholism, primitive types, questions of virility, and infant mortality. It seems to me, however, that Langevin's primary concern has been with communication between human beings. And it is in *Poussière* that he shapes this concern into accomplished art.

A good deal has been written about the book and about Langevin's work in general. The big guns of the Quebec literary scene have all had a go, including Jean-Louis Major (in Volume III of *Archives des lettres canadiennes*), Gilles Marcotte (in his *Une littérature qui se fait*), and Gérard Bessette himself (in *Livres et auteurs québécois*, 1972). Marcotte probably voiced a consensus when he observed that Langevin had furnished "plus de matière à réflexion que la plupart des livres qui ont paru au Canada français depuis quelques années" — *more food for thought than most French-Canadian novels of the last few years.*

What provides the food for thought is André Langevin's intellectual curiosity and his willingness to allow it full rein in his writing. In the last few years there has been bitter controversy about the relative merits of foreign (French, British, American) influences on Canadian writers as opposed to the building up of native traditions through homeborn antecedents. In André Langevin, both characteristics are effectively blended together, which is perhaps the ideal. Since his first book, the critics, Jean-Louis Major in particular, have noted his affinities with Camus and Sartre, his preoccupation with the thematic ideas of existentialism, the confrontation of the self with others, the absurd, and the function of pity in human relations. On the other hand, there are qualities of Langevin's writing which are distinctly Canadian, embracing themes and motifs which can be traced through a number of English- and French-Canadian writers.

The determination of Alain Dubois, hero of *Poussière* to blame himself and to suffer quietly and insistently rather than to strike at the cause of his miseries was, as we have already noted in "The New Hero", a recurrent trait of Canadian protagonists. I call it the *prêtre manqué* syndrome, a legacy of the Calvinist-Jansenist conditioning of people across Canada. Gilles Marcotte's Claude Savoie in *Le Poids de Dieu*, Morley Callaghan's Father Dowling in *Such Is My Beloved*, and Sinclair Ross's Philip Bentley in *As for Me and My House* are obvious examples. Characters who share the same masochistic tendencies can be found in the works of Louis Hémon, Roger Lemelin, Gabrielle Roy, Hugh MacLennan, Hugh Garner, Richard Wright, and numerous others. A real *prêtre manqué*, of course, is a person who would have liked to be a perfect priest, but who has failed for some reason or other and feels guilty thereafter. The same syndrome, however, can be seen in any character, regardless of whether or not he has anything to do with the priesthood, who cannot adapt to the system or to a particular set of circumstances around him and who blames himself rather than the system.

Langevin's Alain Dubois spends a lot of time speculating on what might be wrong with himself, and he punishes himself, even to the extent of permitting his wife to entertain her lover in the public privacy of Dubois' own home, while he sits in his doctor's office listening to her gleeful laughter. Alain Dubois does show defiance, but his defiance is like that of Father Dowling when he ignores the bishop's warnings and continues to help the two prostitutes he has befriended. It is defiance which is guaranteed to increase his own suffering, which is bound to bounce back on him like a rubber ball tossed against a wall. What Dubois defies is the virility principle upheld by the townspeople of Macklin that male dignity, manhood if you will, ought not to be seen to be demeaned. If Alain's wife Madeleine had been having a discreet affair, meeting a lover for weekends in Montreal or Quebec City perhaps, few people would have known, and even those who knew would have smirked and not have been overly concerned. But that she should go alone to Kouri's restaurant and pick up a man, then carry on with him openly, is definitely not acceptable. It is expected that Dubois will take the necessary steps to correct the situation. However much he may think that his married life is his own private business, since Madeleine's conduct is considered an affront to an established concept of manhood, a concept made all the more precious by the erosion of human dignity occasioned by the working conditions of the asbestos mines, her affair becomes a public scandal.

Langevin's triumph of characterization in *Poussière* is his success in engaging the reader's sympathy for Madeleine, despite the fact that the whole story is told from Alain Dubois' point of view. Like George in Hugh MacLennan's *The Watch That Ends the Night*, Dubois is patient and long-suffering, to the point of irritating the average reader perhaps. Madeleine is a bitch by any standards. She is neither abused nor neglected. She can spend what money she likes, even though her husband is in debt. She has a maid, and as a doctor's wife her social status has risen considerably from what it was when she was being brought up in a working-class family. Alain caters to her whims and fancies, including pop music and melo-dramatic movies, neither of which he has much of a stomach for himself. One wishes that Alain would assert himself, would slap down his outrageously brazen wife once in a while at least. As the book progresses, however, one is drawn more and more into seeing Madeleine as Alain sees her and into sharing his emotional reaction to her.

Animal imagery is repeatedly used when Dubois refers to Madeleine. She is called a "jeune fauve" — *wild creature*. She is physically splendid, uninhibited, and sexually potent. Like a cat she is domesticated and wild at the same time, and there is a beauty, a fascination about her wildness. Her acting on impulse and complete unpredictability are a defiance of the drab, humdrum, robot existence of the people around her, and especially of the endless routine of the asbestos miners, who punch the clock and descend into the pits day after day as the shifts change. Like a cat, Madeleine is not capable of submitting to extensive curtailment of her liberty. She cannot be tamed, trained by coercion or bribery to perform tricks on cue. She will not move into line, even as the most undisciplined of the locals, her lover Richard Hétu, eventually does when pressures are brought to bear.

Madeleine is a child in the body of a woman. Somehow she has preserved the innocence, the excitability, the desire for life and adventure of a child. As Alain observes, she wants to try everything, experience everything. The problem, of course, is that even if her husband is willing to let her do so, the community around her is not. Her woman's body disqualifies her from the privileges accorded a child.

Alain's indulgence, moreover, is at first somewhat difficult to comprehend, for he is hardly indifferent to Madeleine. His feelings for her are in fact highly intense, and he is possessive. How can he stand by and allow his wife to be possessed by another? Why should he put up with a woman who will press the accelerator of his car and risk both their lives attempting to beat a train at a level crossing? Why does he permit her to make a fool of him, jeopardizing his self-respect as well as his career? The explanation is there, hinted at on several occasions in the novel. For Alain Dubois, Madeleine is an alter ego. She represents all that he has suppressed in himself. He can hold himself apart from the community around him, he can observe with the eye of a clinician, and he can justify himself by rational argument, as he so effectively does when confronted by the local priest. But Madeleine does not have to hold herself apart, observe, or justify. Her actions are spontaneous, instinctual, like those of a creature of the wild.

Madeleine, thus, symbolizes what regimented man has lost — spontaneity, naturalness, intoxication with life, and delight in novelty, the capacity to treat life as a game. She represents what Alain has lost or perhaps never had. Like the average man, I suppose, he cannot treat life as a game, and he finds his intoxication in alcohol. Cursed with the need to observe and to justify, he must also come to grips with the meaning of life and the question of divine justice. He cannot accept the priest's Jansenist conviction: "Je n'ai jamais cru et je ne croirai jamais au bonheur sur terre." — *I have never believed and will never believe in happiness on earth.* And he has difficulty understanding the philosophical attitude of old Doctor Lafleur, who can accept the world's imperfection and yet still love people enough to continue struggling for whatever small improvements in the human condition are possible.

Langevin succeeds in creating a variety of believable characters in *Poussière*. Besides those already mentioned, there are Kouri, the Syrian owner of a restaurant across the street from the Dubois home, the taxi-driver Jim, the businessman Arthur Prévost, and Thérèse, the maid who works for Madeleine. Together these characters constitute a single character. They are a cross-section of the town of Macklin, the community which Alain and his wife must live with and struggle against, yet each is drawn as an individual with a distinctive personality of his own, a credit to André Langevin's power of characterization.

The author also shows skill in his handling of style, plot, and atmosphere. In translation, of course, one cannot appreciate all the niceties of an author's style, the sentence rhythm and richness of vocabulary for which Langevin has long been praised among French-language critics. One can, nevertheless, note his sensitive use of imagery, especially the animal imagery associated with Madeleine. The structure of the novel is also effective, with significant past events being interwoven through flashbacks into a present-tense, first-person narrative which creates the illusion of immediacy, and in the case of episodes such as the baby delivery and the ending, of dramatic intensity. Having fashioned an introspective, sharply observant doctor as narrator, moreover, Langevin does not have to force in order to incorporate the detail necessary for a convincing atmosphere. The reader sees and feels with Alain Dubois, and he gets to know a Quebec mining town.

In terms of technique and significance of theme, André Langevin's *Poussière sur la ville* is a highly successful novel. It is no wonder that *Le Grand Jury des lettres* declared it the best work of fiction to come out of Quebec in the decade of the 1950s. Taking inspiration from both international literature and local realities, it blends the universal with the regional and acquires an originality of its own.

Also strikingly original is Gérard Bessette's novel *La Bagarre*, but in ways quite different from *Poussière*. Whereas Langevin depicts a psychological drama against the backdrop of a small town, Bessette's novel, published five years later, is a study of a whole society at the threshold of transformation and takes place in the metropolis of Montreal. Unlike André Langevin, who maps out a small territory for minute analysis, Bessette prefers a large expanse. And if his analyses are not as concentrated and penetrating as Langevin's, they are broader in terms of social implication.

Perhaps the best word to describe the career of Gérard Bessette is versatility — versatility of theme, of style, of technique, of genre, and of subject matter. He began with criticism of novels and poetry, then published a collection of his own poems in 1954. His *Les Images en poésie canadienne-française* and *Une Littérature en ébullition* are widely regarded as contemporary classics of literary scholarship, and his *Anthologie d'Albert Laberge* is no doubt responsible for the rediscovery and revival of interest in Laberge, that strange, haunted newspaper sports columnist who published his naturalistic fiction privately and who is the real precursor of such current novelists as Marie-Claire Blais, Réjean Ducharme, and Roch Carrier. Bessette has also written a large body of fiction himself, including six remarkably different novels, two of which, *Le Libraire* and *L'Incubation*, were rendered in English by the translator Glen Shortliffe under the titles *Not For Every Eye* and *Incubation*.

To my mind, however, Bessette's most intriguing book is still his first novel *La Bagarre*, which is now also available in translation — *The Brawl*. In a number of respects this novel foreshadows the major problems and themes which will occupy Quebec society and Quebec authors of the 1960s and since. It is almost uncannily prophetic with regard to labour problems, religion, language, education, and sex, making it even more relevant today, and considerably more meaningful, perhaps, than it was when it first appeared in 1958.

La Bagarre is set in nightclubs around the centre of Montreal, in the streets of the East End and in the old metropolitan tramway car barns at Iberville and Ste. Catherine streets. It concerns a few weeks in the life of Jules Lebeuf, a big, husky 29-year-old man who is working at night as a sweeper in the tramway barns to pay for a belated university education. Lebeuf, whose vague ambition is to become a writer, thus operates in two distinct social circles. He spends a good deal of time drinking in bars with his university friends, Ken Weston, an American ex-GI who is trying to write a thesis on French Canadians, and Augustin Sillery, the sometimes brilliant, spoiled homosexual son of a well-heeled businessman and his refined, aristocratic wife. Lebeuf's mistress, Marguerite, a waitress, and his fellow workers at the tramway barns, on the other hand, are from the lowest level of Quebec's working class. Then there is Gisèle, the pretty, talented daughter of sweeper Philippe "Bill" (unrelated nicknames are sometimes, curiously, used in Quebec) Lafrenière; she has ambitions, and Lebeuf is asked to help her. With such a gallery of characters, Bessette is able to probe the anxieties of individuals in a society at what Lebeuf calls "une croisée de chemins" — *a crossroads*.

And a crossroads it is indeed. Bessette's purpose in *La Bagarre* is to dramatize the upheaval resulting when a long-suppressed, static, conservative group of people, mainly rural-oriented, suddenly find themselves in the frantic, cosmopolitan, rapidly changing North American urban context. For centuries in Quebec, the roles which individuals would follow in life were established and well defined. And the mechanisms were there to keep everyone in line, as illustrated throughout *Poussière sur la ville*, especially when Madeleine's lover, Richard, is pressured into abandoning his sport with the doctor's wife and marrying an appropriate local girl. But in Bessette's world, a society where the Old Order is disintegrating, the roles have become indefinite and confused. Sillery, from the social class of the former *collège-classique*-educated elite of Quebec, has difficulty understanding how Lebeuf can be a student in arts and yet sweep out tramcars for a living. Lebeuf's fellow workers are mystified by the phenomenon of a sweeper attending courses at l'Université de Montréal. Nobody, including Lebeuf, is adjusted to the new mobility and freedom. In fact, freedom and how various individuals react to it, are essentially what Gérard Bessette's *La Bagarre* is about. Contrary to some popular slogans, since the 1950s Quebec has steadily become a freer and freer society.

The various forces which acted in concert to suppress individual liberty in French Canada — the church, the caste system, ingrained attitudes towards sex and education, labour-management relations — all of these are shown by Bessette at a stage of weakening or modification, another world completely from that of *Poussière sur la ville*. The protagonist, Jules Lebeuf, is an example of the "liberated" individual. He has travelled and worked in the United States, but he has come home to realize his ambitions. He lives with Marguerite without benefit of clergy. He also goes back to school, where the only person in his age group turns out to be the American, Weston.

He takes Gisèle to a psychologist for an aptitude test, and when it is established that she has an exceptional talent for mathematics, he advises her to take a part-time job and study at Sir George Williams College, despite the pressures on her either to go to work in a factory or to follow an unsuitable classical course at a convent.

Among his fellow workers at the tramway barns, Lebeuf is the leader. Bessette paints a fascinating group portrait of the other workers, old Onésime Boulé, known as "Bouboule", Bill, Charlot the Italian, the fat Marceau, *le père* Breton, and the person hated by them all, Lévêque the foreman. The men constantly curse the company ("ces maudits écoeurants d'enfants-de-chienne-là") in general and, because he is immediately available, Lévêque in particular. They talk of striking, but in fact, as Bessette subtly demonstrates, they are helpless. They do not really know what to do. They fear authority. They have been conditioned, as their fathers and grandfathers before them were, to accept misery as their lot. When old Bouboule finally erupts, he foolishly and ineffectually hits the foreman on the head with a broom. As a result, he loses his job and his pension is cancelled, after thirty years of service!

Bouboule, thus, is like Philip Bentley in *As for Me and My House*, the type of the old Canadian hero. It is Lebeuf, half-way there to the "new hero" discussed earlier, who intercedes for Bouboule, the other men again proving themselves incapable of positive action. And it is only by accepting the offer to replace Lévêque as foreman, thus divorcing himself from his old co-workers, that Lebeuf is able to get the company to reinstate Bouboule, who thereafter becomes a model employee.

The company, then, wins the first round by a unanimous decision. The threat, the potential trouble-maker, is shifted from one side of the fence to the other. But as Bessette intimates, the real problem with regard to the exploitation of labour in Quebec is not so much the attitude of management (bosses will bend when they have to); rather it is the ingrained subservience of the workers ("ces mines de chiens battus"). What is of greater significance, however, is that leaders who have shaken off this inferiority complex are emerging. There are the Lebeufs, and not all of them will be lifted over the fence. The situation is ripe for explosion. Bessette, therefore, accurately predicts the massive unrest and resulting conflicts which have hit Quebec labour relations in the years following the publication of *La Bagarre*. And he provides a perceptive analysis of the whole spectrum of attitudes — servile acceptance, fear, dissatisfaction, indirection, blind defiance, futile violence, recrimination, and reasoned determination — which continue to characterize the phenomenon. One need look no further than *La Bagarre* to understand why management-labour relations in Quebec have followed such a rocky road.

Bessette's novel also heralds the collapse of the influence of the church in Quebec. For most of the characters, including Lebeuf, Marguerite, and Augustin, religion is no longer a consideration at all. Marguerite, it is true, makes a vestigial concession to the Old Order when she buys an "alliance" (a wedding ring) before visiting the doctor for a pregnancy check, but it is obviously in the interests of convenience rather than morality. Langevin's Alain Dubois and Madeleine may also be said to be not especially religious from all appearances, but despite their indifference the local priest still manages to control major aspects of their lives in one way or another. No such control is evident in *La Bagarre*. Bill's reason for consulting Lebeuf about Gisèle's future is that he doesn't trust the local priests — "ils voudraient qu'elle fasse eine soeur" — *they want to make a nun out of her*, he says. As it turns out, Bill trusts "les maudzits Anglais" even less. When Lebeuf suggests that Gisèle pursue her studies at an English-speaking college, he hesitates, and Gisèle ends up at a convent after all. But it is Bill's fear that his daughter will marry "English" rather than his allegiance to the church which conditions his decision, or indecision.

In Quebec novels before *La Bagarre*, the church is regarded in two general ways: earlier works by such authors as Conan, Gérin-Lajoie, Grignon, Hémon, or Ringuet show it dominating the lives of all and never being seriously questioned; it is an accepted fact of life. Beginning with Albert Laberge and Jean-Charles Harvey and moving on to Simard, Roy, Marcotte, and André Langevin, we see a struggle between church values and the individual's personal sense of ethics. *La Bagarre* stands at the crossroads. In it there is no struggle against the church; more often than not, the church as a life-moulding force simply is not there. Which, of course, is the shape of things to come in the recent works of such writers as Godbout, Aquin, Poulin, and a number of others.

What Bessette captures in *La Bagarre*, then, is Quebec at the crucial period of transformation from a static society to a dynamic society. Traditional attitudes are lingering on, but it is clear that they are of rapidly fading importance in the minds of the people. The major problem is that the people do not know what to do with their newly acquired freedom. It has come about too quickly. The workers at the tramway barns do not go much further than mumbling vague threats about strike action. Though her parents want a life better than their own for Gisèle, they are afraid to stray too far from the familiar pattern. Gisèle herself is unsure. Marguerite is willing to "live in sin" with Lebeuf, but secretly she yearns for the supposed security of marriage and a small motel near the American border which she and Jules can operate together. Bill looks upon the cohabitation of Marguerite and Jules with admiration and relish, but he presumes that Lebeuf will eventually drop his mistress and find a "decent" girl to marry. Finally, Lebeuf himself proves incapable of resolving his own life. He wants to be a writer, but he constantly finds excuses not to write, because he is afraid that he will fail. He wants a university degree, yet he quits when only a few weeks' work would earn him one. He wants to remain a worker with the other workers, but he accepts the job as foreman. At the climax of the book, because he does not like the idea of the 16-year-old Gisèle in a nightclub with Augustin Sillery, he precipitates a senseless brawl, fighting clients and waiters and being saved from a beer-bottle blow to the head by his friend Weston. Lebeuf thus becomes the symbol of a society in transition, of the indirection resulting from the disappearance of old values and patterns of living, and of the potential for a particular kind of violent eruption in Quebec. He is a complex, confused character, just as Quebec in the current period of transition is complex and confused. It is no wonder that Weston, the American who has come to write a thesis on French Canadians, finally decides that the task is impossible and goes home to a newspaper job in Saint Louis.

In addition to its thematic significance, *La Bagarre* is distinguished by other qualities. Characterization, both major and minor, is executed with skill and sensitivity. Of particular note is Augustin Sillery, possibly the first complete and convincing portrait of a homosexual in Canadian literature. Sillery is refined and well informed, a man of exquisite taste in certain respects, and he is able to parlay these qualities into acceptance by the intellectual group within which he moves. In fact, he parades his effeminacy, delicately raising his cigarette holder, exaggerating his gestures, calling everyone "mon cher", frequently alluding to homosexuality in one way or another. When Lebeuf does the same satirically, Sillery comes right back with a remark about the latter's non-existent writings — "Si jamais tu daignais soumettre à mes yeux fascinés quelques lignes de ta plume, je me prosternerais front contre terre et admirerais en silence" — and usually that is enough to silence the big man.

Sillery's relationship with his mother and father is carefully delineated by Bessette. The father is a hard-headed businessman who does not know what to make of his only son. Consequently there is little communication between the two. Augustin's mother, on the other hand, dotes on him. She waits up until all hours for him to come home, and to the exclusion of the father, she has constructed her life around his comings and goings. She must have a fair idea that he is homosexual, yet she keeps hoping that he will become involved with the right girl. At the same time, it is clear that she would not want to lose her son to another woman. Whether or not a contributing cause of his homosexuality, Augustin's relationship with his mother has obviously not militated against it.

The intensity of Augustin's emotions, especially with regard to a young student (coincidentally called Langevin), is impressed repeatedly on the reader. Particularly effective is the scene where Augustin, infuriated by Langevin's failure to show up for a rendez-vous, tries to pick up a youth at a bowling alley. The youth is with another couple, and Sillery seems repulsed by the girl — "un animal à reproduction". But when the girl bends over in her tight skirt, displaying the shape of her ample buttocks, he thinks to himself, "Dire qu'il existe des hommes pour trouver ça provocant! Sillery les enviait." He envies the men who can react normally to women. In other words, despite his appearance of arrogant confidence, Sillery has deep feelings of insecurity and guilt. Quebec society has not yet changed sufficiently for it to be otherwise, and like Weston, Augustin Sillery finally decides to leave the province. Bessette succeeds in presenting the complexities of Augustin's personality in the same way that André Langevin succeeds with the simple, childlike, forcefully heterosexual Madeleine, engaging the reader's sympathies when the opposite might have been the more expected reaction — altogether an adroit and convincing piece of characterization.

Bessette's technique of characterization relies heavily on dialogue, differing from Langevin's reliance on internal monologue. There are a number of revealing and entertaining interchanges between Lebeuf and Marguerite, or among Weston, Sillery, and Lebeuf. The most striking aspect of Bessette's style in *La Bagarre* is his handling of the spoken language, whether the "joual" of the tramway sweepers, the schoolgirl French of Gisèle, the not-completely-learned variety of Weston, or the affected diction of Augustin. Here, for instance, is the latter talking to Lebeuf and Weston: "Rien messieurs, ne me réchaufferait davantage le coeur que de poursuivre jusqu'à l'aurore aux doigts de rose ces palabres marécageuses, mais de devoirs impérieux me requièrent en d'autres lieux." — *Nothing, gentlemen, would more warm my heart than to pursue these marshy palavers until the rosy-fingered dawn, but imperative duties call me elsewhere* (p. 58).

Now compare Sillery's language with that of the sweepers: "Watch out, les boys. Je vois le fanal de Lévêque. Il s'en vient de ce côté-icitte. On est mieux de scrammer." — *Watch out, boys. I see Lévêque's lamp. He's coming over this way. We better beat it* (p. 49). And there are many variations between these two extremes.

Strangely enough, Gérard Bessette, who has proven himself so adept at handling many levels of the spoken language, considers, or at least used to consider the linguistic problem to be the biggest obstacle facing French-Canadian writers. In a commentary on the Quebec novel, he remarks on the success of the Americans in establishing their own brand of English. Then he goes on to say:

> Will we French-Canadian novelists ever enjoy the same independence, the same feeling of linguistic power? I think not. What would actually be required? Nothing less than a population and political, cultural, and military influence comparable to those of France. (This is the case of the United States vis-à-vis England.) Short of that we are not able (we cannot even wish) to allow our language to evolve "naturally". For that would be to replace a "universal" language with a dialect.[13]

This statement was made some ten years ago, and it is possible that Bessette has now become more optimistic with regard to the possibility of Quebec French gaining respectability and legitimacy as a vehicle for literary expression. Certainly in the last ten years or so a number of writers have been moving steadily in that direction, as shown in the second essay of this volume. With regard to both the art of writing and the use of the language of Quebec, there is now a great deal more self-assurance and confidence. When he wrote *La Bagarre*, Gérard Bessette stood with André Langevin and a small number of others at the forefront of the new literary sensibility of Quebec. That sensibility is now firmly established, as the variety, quality, and fertility of contemporary writing attest, and the works of Langevin and Bessette must be regarded as large and important contributing factors.

YVON DESCHAMPS –
NEW LIFE FOR THE OLD MONOLOGUE

A bouncy, impish little man called Yvon Deschamps is quite probably the most popular performer in Quebec today, and he is a good reason for Gérard Bessette to have confidence in the power of Quebec French, even at its most unrefined spoken level, to convey subtleties. In terms of professional category, I suppose one might say that Deschamps is a stand-up comedian, and certainly he can hold audiences spellbound for as long as he likes. He always plays to packed houses, and his two record albums have sold more than 100,000 copies each.

But Yvon Deschamps is much more than a flash-in-the-pan comedian. He is a literary phenomenon (Éditions Leméac has brought out a book of his monologues from 1968 to 1973), an exponent of the oldest and perhaps the most influential genre in Canada, and I suspect that it is in literary terms that his true merit will eventually be judged.

In a highly perceptive article called "Le Monologue québécois" (published in *Canadian Literature* 58), scholar Laurent Mailhot examines the work of Yvon Deschamps from the viewpoint of the monologue tradition, at the same time explaining the native significance of the tradition. Mailhot sees the monologue taking firm hold and flourishing in Quebec because of "certains aspects de notre géographie et de notre histoire: l'isolement des rangs et des fermes, la rigueur de l'hiver, la longueur des voyages, l'exil saisonnier des forestiers." He goes on to point out that numerous vital works of literature, including plays such as Barbeau's *Solange*, Maillet's *La Sagouine*, and Tremblay's *Les Belles-soeurs*, are in fact offshoots of the traditional monologue, the standard entertainment of long winter nights in isolated rural communities.

Now it seems to me that Laurent Mailhot may well be on to something, and not only for Quebec writing but for that of the whole of Canada. After all, the nights were just as long and cold and the rural communities just as isolated in the rest of Canada as in Quebec. Is it possible that Canadian writers in general are more adept at using the monologue — first-person narration in colloquial diction where mood and often ironic self-analysis and observation are more important than plot — than other literary techniques? Does the monologue somehow strike an especially responsive chord in Canadians? In Quebec, as Mailhot suggests, the answer seems definitely to be positive. Besides the plays already mentioned and numerous other dramatic works, there are novels such as Réjean Ducharme's *L'Avalée des avalés*, Hubert Aquin's *Prochain épisode*, as well as André Langevin's *Poussière sur la ville*, which are essentially monologues. But one thinks also of well-known books written in English — Sinclair Ross's *As for Me and My House*, Robertson Davies' *Fifth Business*, large sections in the work of Hugh MacLennan, Leonard Cohen, Margaret Laurence, W. O. Mitchell, and Richard Wright.

On the other hand, American classics such as *Huckleberry Finn* and *Moby Dick* also borrow from the monologue tradition. Perhaps the phenomenon, if indeed it has any significance at all, is North American rather than Canadian. Whatever the case, Yvon Deschamps, the Quebec entertainer, is unquestionably a monologuist, and he is breathing new life into an old form.

It has been suggested that since Deschamps uses colloquial Montreal French, or "joual" as it is sometimes called, the great majority of anglophone Canadians will not be able to understand him. Certainly when performing on the stage Deschamps speaks rapidly, interspersing his texts with sounds, songs, gestures, and ad-libs, making no concessions to standards of accent and grammar other than his own — he is, of course, speaking the language of the workingman he portrays. Nevertheless, an examination of Deschamps's monologues in their printed form, despite certain inconsistencies in the texts, reveals that the man himself is reasonably consistent. As in the spoken language itself, words, expressions, and phrases are often repeated, and once the reader has mastered a few basic patterns, the diction of Yvon Deschamps is hardly as challenging as it would seem at first sight.

For example, *qu'est-ce que ça* (what?) will be elided to *quossa*, as in the expression *quossa donne*, the equivalent of the English "Whatta yuh get out of it?" or "Whatta they good fer?" *Moé* and *toé* (pronounced "*mway*" and "*tway*") are standard *moi* and *toi*. *Il* and *la* are often shortened to *y* and *à*, *puis* to *pis*; the *e* is elided in a number of words (*s'maine* for *semaine*, *p'tit* for *petit*, etc.) and the *r* in others (*autes* for *autres*, *not* for *notre*, etc.). Sometimes the vowel in words like *chercher* and *merde* will be modified so that the words become *charcher* and *marde*. And that's about it. Aware of these devices, the reader with a high-school knowledge of standard French ought to be able, I believe, to read Yvon Deschamps. For practice here is the beginning of the first monologue he performed, the one which accidentally launched his career. It is called "Les Unions, quossa donne?" — *Unions, Whatta They Good Fer?*

Non, mais c'est vrai, par exemple quand tu y penses, les unions, quossa donn? Ça donne rien . . . c'est vrai. . . . On n'a tu une union à shop, nous autes? On n'a pas. Moé, ça fait 15 ans que j'travaille à shop . . . ça fait 15 ans qu'y a pas d'union. Quossa donne?

On n'a pas d'union, pis ça empêche pas que depuis à s'maine passée, on a à s'maine de 54 heures. Pis, on a not congé à Noël ou ben donc au Jour de l'An . . . pis l'été, on a une s'maine de vacances payées. On la prend pas toujours, mais ça fait rien, on l'a pareil. . . . Aye, pis moé, ça paraît pas, mais j'fais des s'maines de $62, 63, pis déjà avec d'l'overtime, chus t'allé m'charcher $73 . . . pas clair.

Quand j'ai laché école à 13 ans, mon vieux pére, y était sus son lit d'mort, y dit . . . mon p'tit garçon, j'peux pas t'laisser d'héritage. . . . m'en doutait un peu, à vitesse qu'y buvait . . . Mais seulement avant d'partir, j'peux t'dire que dans à vie y a deux choses qui comptent . . . une job steady, pis un bon boss. Les maudites affaires d'union, quossa donne, ça? Une job steady, pis un bon boss. Pis, là, y é parti. (p. 19)

No, but it's true, fer instance, when yuh think about it, unions, whatta they good fer? Nothin' . . . it's true. . . . Have we got a union at the shop, us? We have not. Me, 15 years I've bin workin' at the shop . . . 15 years that we got no union. Whatta they good fer?

We got no union, but that ain't stopped us from gettin' a 54-hour week, since a week ago. Besides, we got our Christmas holiday, or else New Years' . . . an' in summer we get a week's vacation with pay. We don't take it all the time, but that's all right — we get it jus' the same. An' me eh, it may not look it, but some weeks I make $62, $63, an' already with overtime I've picked up $73 . . . not clear.

When I quit school at 13, my old dad, he was on his deathbed, he says . . . my little son, I ain't got nothin' to leave yuh. . . . I figgered as much, the rate he usta booze it up . . . but before I go, I can only tell yuh that in life there's two things that count . . . a steady job an' a good boss. That damned union business what's it good fer? A steady job an' a good boss. An' then, he was gone.

The beginning of Deschamps's first monologue quoted above provides a good idea of his method and subject matter. Usually he presents himself as the typical Quebec workingman, much like the tramway men in Gérard Bessette's *La Bagarre*, trying to cope with the life around him — his job, the unions, the English, television, sex, movies, and so on. But the character is more than just that, much more — he is also the universal little man confronting twentieth-century North America: violence, confusion of values, indirection, prejudices, hatred, war, solitude, and rapid change. And since narrator Deschamps is the little man, he also embodies many of the weaknesses and human deficiencies of individuals in our society. The laughter turns in upon himself. Complaining about the horrors of intolerance and prejudice, for example, it turns out that he is unwittingly and hopelessly intolerant and prejudiced himself: "Ouan, mais c'est vrai, l'intolérance, c'est pas tolérable." — *Yeah, but it's true, intolerance shouldn't be tolerated.* Then being on the subject, he goes on to list all the other things which should not be tolerated, wondering why we put up with them: "Moé, j'dis, les tapettes, les lesbiennes, les affaires comme ça, on devrait pas tolérer ça dans une société normale, on devrait toute sacrer ça en prison. Toute!" — *Me, I say, fairies, lesbians, all that kind of stuff, we shouldn't stand for that in a normal society. We oughta slap 'em all in jail. All of 'em!*

As an aside and a typical Deschamps topical dig, incidentally, in the monologue on intolerance he mentions that Prime Minister Pierre Trudeau has passed laws to protect homosexuals and wonders what will happen next. "Pis comme j'connais M. Trudeau," he says, "pour gagner ses prochaines élections, y ben capable de légaliser l'avortement pour les tapettes." — *An' if I know Mr. Trudeau, to win the next election he's quite capable of legalizin' abortion for fairies.*

Deschamps, the little-man narrator, is at once abused and abusing, selfish and generous, perceptive at moments but often naive. He is the product of a mixed-up, ailing society. We laugh at him, we laugh with him, we sympathize with him, we detest him, but more often than not we see in him something of ourselves, and it is not always a pleasant experience. If we did not laugh, we might feel inclined to cry.

Sometimes he uses the ignorance and naiveness of his character to give a monologue an ironic twist. "Nigger Black" is a good example:

Nigger black . . . nigger black . . .
nigger black. . . . Moé, quand j'tais
p'tit, on voyait des nègres, on leu
criait ça . . . nigger black. Non,
mais c'est parce que quand on
était p'tit, on était jaloux des
nègres, nous autes . . . c'est parce
qu'on trouvait que y étaient
chanceux, eux autes. Aye, y étaient
toute frisés, y avaient pas besoin
d'se peigner. Y pouvaient pas
attraper d'coups d'soleil . . . ça
paraissait pas quand y étaient
sales. (p. 37)

Nigger black . . . nigger black
. . . nigger black. . . . Me, when I
was a kid, we'd see a negro an'
we'd shout that . . . nigger black.
No, well it's cause when we was
kids we was jealous of negroes, us
guys . . . cause we figgered they
was lucky, those guys was.
Their hair was all curly eh, so's
they didn't have to comb it.
They couldn't get sunburnt . . .
an' it didn't show when they
got dirty.

And the monologue goes on from there, making the audience acutely aware of the problems that blacks have to endure in the theoretically liberal metropolis of Montreal.

Deschamps's satire can be poignant and bitter, but it can also be light-hearted, poking fun rather than punching holes. "Le p'tit Jésus" is in the second category, a humorous parody of simplistic religion, the non-thinking acceptance of everything one is told. In many ways it is reminiscent of the speeches of Saint Sammy in W .O. Mitchell's novel *Who Has Seen the Wind*. Retelling the story of Jesus from the point of view of an uneducated and uninformed workingman, Deschamps comes up with an ingenious transformation into current language and concepts, again striking out at numerous prejudices and stupidities along the way.

After describing the birth and early years of Jesus, Deschamps tells how he attempts to gather around him a "grosse gang". But Jesus annoys people, especially since he insists on talking about his father all the time — "mon pére par ci, mon pére par là, mon pére a faite ci. . . ." Then the monologue continues:

C'est pas pour ça qu'le monde
l'aimait pas. Le monde l'aimait pas,
premièrement, ben c'tait un Juif,
et pis he, à part de t'ça, y avait
une grande barbe, t'sais, fait que
y pouvait pas rentrer n'importe
you. . . . Et pis, lui y aimait ça
porter les ch'veux sus é
z'épaules . . . fait que presque

That wasn't why people
didn't like 'im. People didn't
like 'im, first, well he was a Jew;
an' then besides that, he had a big
beard, yuh know, which meant
that he couldn't get in to jus'
anyplace. An' then he liked that,
wearin' his hair down to his
shoulders . . . which meant that all

toutes les troubles y passaient sus
l'dos. Ben c'est surtout parce qu'y
avait une manie ben fatigante . . .
énarvante . . . y ramassait des
grosses gangs, t'sais . . .
pis là ça marchait dans é rues . . .
pis, on va changer ci, pis on va
changer ça, le monde
haïssait ça. Dans c'temps-là
le monde comprenait pas — c'tait
pas comme aujourd'hui. Y
comprenaient tellement pas qu'le
grand prêtre en chef, un moment
donné, a dit: pus d'marchage dans
é rues en gang . . . en plein
Dgérousalem. . . . j'te dis qu'c'est
grave, ça.

Ça fait que quand Jésus-Christ
a vu ça, y a emmené sa gang sus
une colline pour parlementer.
Ça fait que y a monté sus une
grosse roche, y dit: Les gars,
finies les folies! Pierre, viens
ici, pis Jean-Jacques, farme-toé,
pis écoute. Pierre, tu es Pierre?
L'aute y dit oui.
Pierre, tu es Pierre —
vous l'avez dit ça —
Ben laisse-moé parler,
m'a t'sacrer une claque.
Pierre, tu es Pierre, et Pierre
qui roule n'amasse pas mousse.
Non mais de toutes façons, l'aute
a pas compris, parce que y en un
qui parlait en hébreu, l'aute
parlait en paraboles. (pp. 69–70)

*kinds of troubles landed on his
back. Well mostly it was 'cause
he had a very annoyin' habit . . .
nerve-wrackin' . . . he used to get
together big gangs, yuh know . . .
then they'd march in the streets
. . . they was gonna change this,
they was gonna change that, and
people hated that. In those days,
people didn't understand — it
wasn't like nowadays. They
didn't understand so much that
the big chief priest at one
time said: no more marchin' in
the streets in gangs . . . in the
middle of Jeruslum. I'm tellin'
yuh it's a serious business, that.*

*So when Jesus Christ
saw that, he took his gang up
a hill to figger things out.
So he got up on a big rock
an' he says: You guys, no
more fun an' games! Peter, come
here, an' John-James, shut up an'
listen. Peter, are you the Stone?
The other he says yes.
Peter, are you the Stone?
Yuh just said that —
Well lemme talk, will yuh,
or I'll smack you one.
Peter, you are the Stone, an' a
rollin' stone gathers no moss.
No, well, anyhow, the other guy
didn't get it, 'cause one of 'em
was speakin' in Hebrew an' the
other was speakin' in parables.*

Jesus goes on to explain to the disciples that they should love one
another, despite the fact that "la loi était pas passée" — *the law
hasn't been passed.* Then he tries to outline the policy of turning the
other cheek:

A partir d'aujourd'hui, si quelqu'un
vous tape, han, au lieu d'vous

*From now on, if somebody
clobbers yuh, eh, well instead*

r'venger, vous allez leur	*of fightin' back, yuh're gonna*
demander de vous taper encore!	*ask 'em to clobber yuh again!*
Les gars étaient pas d'accord,	*The guys didn't agree,*
c'tait pas des canayens français	*they wasn't French Canajuns,*
ça, c'tait des Juifs.	*those guys, they was Jews.*

Deschamps ends the monologue by discovering the reason why Christ's birthday is no longer celebrated the way it should be — the problem is that it falls during the Christmas holidays, when everyone is busy. But the infallible Pope refuses to change the date, so if people "aiment mieux vivre comme des païens" — *would rather live like pagans* — "ben y ont rinque une affaire à faire" — *well they got only one thing to do* — "qu'y prennent leur pilule" — *swallow the pill.*

There is, of course, a good deal of black humour in Yvon Deschamps's monologues, when he talks about the treatment of the aged, for example, or in "Cable TV", which dwells upon people's fascination with the morbid — bloody violence, crime, fatal accidents, and the like. Generally he moves from the particular to the universal, launching a monologue around some personal matter or a current issue in Quebec. "Le p'tit Jésus", as we have seen, dramatizes the trend since the 1960s away from subservience to the church. Another piece, "Histoire du Canada", reflects the current propensity among scholars and historians to debunk traditional concepts of Canadian history.

The monologue begins by Deschamps commenting on a history book which his son has nipped from school. He leafs through the book, *Histoire du Canada*, as he progresses, referring to page numbers from time to time:

Ça commence très bien,	*It starts out good, the*
Histoire du Canada, ça commence,	History of Canada, *it starts,*
ça commence tu suite, là on ouvre	*right away, right where yuh open*
le couvert . . . bon, ça commence.	*the cover . . . good, so it starts.*
C'est des Français de France qu'on	*It's some French of France that*
commencé ça. R'marquez qu'c'est	*starts it all. Notice that it's*
toujours des Français de France	*always some French of France*
qui commencent toute. Ben pas	*that starts everythin'. Well not*
toujours. Mais c'est toujours	*always. But that's always*
l'impression qu'ça donne quand	*the impression yuh get when*
c'est eux-autres qui l'expliquent	*they's the ones explainin' it,*
en té cas. Ça, c'était des Français	*in any case. It was some French*
de France qui sontaient en France.	*of France that lived in France.*
Ça, c'était dans l'temps qu'y	*That was when there was still*

restaient un peu là-bas. Ça
fait que y en avait une gang
qu'était là, y en avait une gang
qu'avait pas de job steady
ça fait que y en a un qui r'garde
les autres, y dit: Comme qu'on a
pas de job steady, pourquoi s'qu'on
fait pas comme les autres qu'ont
pas de job steady, pourquoi s'qu'on
s'en va-pas-t-au Canada? Les
autres ont dit: C't'une bonne idée
qu't'a là.
  Là moé, j'vous parle dans l'temps
que les jobs icitte, y en avait.
Ah oui, ça, c'est ben avant M.
Bourassa, on é à page deux à peu
près. Fait que les gars sont partis
de dlà, sont arrivés icitte, à page
trois. Sont arrivés moé j'pensais
qu'y étaient arrivés dans l'boutte
d'la Gaspésie, des affaires de
même, mais en le r'lisant, j'me sus-
t-aperçu que je m'étais trompé,
sont arrivés à Montréal direct.
Oui, c'é écrit sus à page trois,
sont arrivés par le pont Jacques
Cartier. Oui, là y ont descendu
la rue Delormier . . . non, ça c'est
pas écrit, mais crime, c'est un
one-way, y avaient pas le choix.
(pp. 147–48)

a few of 'em over there. It
happened that there was a gang
of 'em there, there was a gang of
'em that didn't have no steady
jobs. So one of 'em looks at the
others an' he says: Since we ain't
got no steady jobs, why don't
we do like the others that ain't
got steady jobs, why don't
we go to Canada? The others said:
That's a good idea yuh got
there.
  Now me, I'm talkin to yuh
about a time when there was jobs
here. Oh yeah, that was a long
time before Mr. Bourassa: we're
on page two about. So the guys
left there an' arrived here, on
page three. I usta think, me, that
they arrived somewhere around
the Gaspé, or somethin' like that,
but readin' about it again I
could see that I was wrong,
they came to Montreal direct.
Sure, it's written on page three,
they came over the Jacques
Cartier Bridge. Sure, then they
came down Delormier Street . . .
no, that's not written, but cripes,
it's a one-way, they didn't have
no choice.

The French meet "une gang de sauvages", and they are struck with
terror. But the French are no fools. They bring out large mirrors,
and since the Indians look terrifying, when they see their own
reflections in the mirrors they terrify themselves. "Non, mais ça,
c'est normal," says Deschamps, "parce que ça fait toujours peur la
première fois que tu te vois tel que t'es." — *No, but that, that's only*
normal, because yuh're always frightened the first time yuh see
yerself as yuh really are.
  The monologue continues, touching upon the exploitation of the
Indians, the Conquest and various other events of the past. The
tendency toward xenophobia in French Canada does not escape
Deschamps's jabs:

Parce que nous autes, les Canayens français, si on a une qualité, c'est pas sûr encore, mai si on n'a une, c'est ben celle d'aimer tout le monde. On haït pas parsonne.

J'parle du vrai monde là, pas les Anglais. Non, ça, ok, les Anglais, on les haït, ça c'est correct. Les Français aussi. Les Pollocks, les Italiens, les Russes, Les Américains, les Chinois, les Japonais, les Tchécoslovaques, les Cubains, bon, les nègres, et pis, bon, les Hindoux. Mais à part de ça, à part de ça, on aime tout le monde. (p. 155)

'Cause us, French Canajuns, if there's one good thing about us — which ain't sure yet — but if there is one, well it's that we love everybody. We don't hate nobody.

I'm speakin' 'bout real people now, not the English. No, ok, the English, we hate 'em — that's all right. The French too. The Polacks, Italians, Russians, Americans, Chinese, Japanese, Czechoslovakians, Cubans, right, Negroes, an' then, right, the Hindus. But outside of that, outside of that, we love everybody.

Actually, Quebeckers, among whom Deschamps is so popular, certainly bear the brunt of his satiric thrusts. He hits hard and often, and seldom does he pull his punches. At the end of "Histoire du Canada", he gets around to the October Crisis of 1970:

Pis en octobre 70, vous vous en rappelez pas d'octobre 70? La grosse crise d'octobre? Qu'on souffrait toute dans not sécurité? Ça veut dire qu'on shakait dans nos culottes. Bon. Crime, on n'osait pus sortir dehors tellement qu'on avait peur. Y en a-tu un Anglais qu'y s'en é aperçu? Pas un maudit. A fallu encore que ça soye des Canayens français: M. Drapeau, M. Bourassa, M. Trudeau, qui s'aperçoivent qu'on avait peur. Qui passent la loi des mesures de guerre, pour nous aider. Qui nous envoient l'armée pour nous protéger. Qui mettent le plus d'monde en prison pour qu'on soye tranquille. N'importe qui, envoye, en masse. Bon. Bang. Bang. Y a pas un Anglais qu'aurait faite ça pour nous autes!

Then in October 70, yuh don't remember October 70? The big October crisis? When our security was all messed up? Meanin' that we was shakin' in our britches. Right. Cripes, we was so afraid we didn't dare go out any more. Was there an Englishman that noticed? Not a damned one. Once again it had to be French Canajuns, Mr. Drapeau, Mr. Bourassa, Mr. Trudeau, that notices that we was afraid. That passes the War Measures Act to help us out. That sends in the Army to protect us. That puts the most people in prison so's we can feel calm. Anybody, round 'em up, the works. Right. Bang. Bang. There ain't an Englishman that woulduv done that fer us! No, an' I'll tell yuh

Non, ben m'a vous dire rinqu'un
affaire. Douglas, pis Stanfield à
Ottawa, c'est des Anglais, ben ces
écoeurants-là, y étaient contre
la loi des mesures de guerre. Faut
qu'y nous haïssent assez! (p. 160)

*jus' one thing. Douglas, then
Stanfield in Ottawa, they's
English, them damned rotters,
they was against the War
Measures Act. They must really
hate us!*

Yvon Deschamps, thus, is more than a mere entertainer. His
monologues are indeed funny, but they are also loaded with a great
deal of perceptive commentary — on contemporary affairs, on
society, on human nature, and on the human condition. Obviously
it is too soon to make a pronouncement on the literary merit and
durability of Deschamps's work. Will its splashes of the universal be
able to sustain that which is strictly topical and dated? Already he
has imitators. Will the ancient form of the monologue now take on
new life, encroaching upon the preserves of poetry and fiction, yet
at the same time reaching the masses of people who generally ignore
"serious" literature?

THE RELEVANCE OF ROBERTSON DAVIES

I must confess that I always found novelist, dramatist, and essayist
Robertson Davies something of an enigma. Having once heard him
address, purportedly in the interests of national bilingualism, a
convocation at Bishop's University entirely in Latin, I was never
certain when to take Davies seriously. He did not fit into any of the
general thematic patterns of Canadian writing as I saw them,
which, of course, was perfectly all right. His works are of high
literary merit, glitteringly clever, witty, and entertaining — that they
have been somewhat distinctive in the body of Canadian literature
only adds to their merit perhaps.

As a humorist, Robertson Davies seems to me to be very British,
a complete contrast to Yvon Deschamps. The North American
tradition of literary humour — I am not sure if there is a peculiarly
Canadian variety — can be traced back through the comedy writers
of American newspapers of the early 1800s and Mark Twain to
Thomas Chandler Haliburton. This tradition leans heavily on dialect
or accent (German and Italian immigrants used to be favourite
targets: Mudder, may I a swimming went? Nix, mine grosse dotter;

What's a specimen? An Italian astronaut.), incongruity, exaggeration, and the naive or "queer" character to achieve humorous effect. Almost any of Mark Twain's best-known works would serve to illustrate — the use of several dialects in *Huckleberry Finn*, the naiveness of Jim, the exaggeration of Romanticism in the Shepherdson-Grangerford episode, the incongruity of the "Duke" and the "King", and so on. The same devices also characterize the humour of Canadian specialists such as Stephen Leacock, Henry Drummond, Paul Hiebert, W. O. Mitchell, or Yvon Deschamps. Leacock's sketches sparkle with the comedy of slight exaggeration and incongruity, and Drummond's verse depends entirely on the fractured English of the French-Canadian habitant. Hiebert, Mitchell, and Deschamps, all three exploit dialect (Mitchell's Saint Sammy and Jake are prime examples) and the naiveness or oddness of characters. Paul Hiebert's delightful *Sarah Binks* might well have been inspired by Mark Twain's storied spoof review of the "Sweet Singer of Michigan" (who, incidentally, took the review seriously and wrote another book), and certainly Hiebert uses the device of exaggeration with brilliant results. Yvon Deschamps's monologues, as we have seen, often build upon the incongruous, such as in the retelling of the story of "le p'tit Jésus", with his "grosse gang", hippie beard, and annoying habit of demonstrating in the streets against one thing or another.

Now I realize that it is unsafe to make such generalizations, and surely there will be many exceptions, but I see the devices of British humour to be for the most part quite different from those of the North American tradition. In Britain, for instance, dialects are used to identify, but apparently they have been around too long to be funny in themselves. Even in something like George Bernard Shaw's *Pygmalion*, dialect, I suspect, adds colour rather than comedy for the Britisher. It was in the United States that the play was made into such an immensely popular musical. Difficult it is to imagine Scottish, Irish, Welsh, or English diction being used in the same way as W. O. Mitchell uses Saint Sammy's speech in the following, where Sammy is telling about God warning him of a storm:

> Sammy, Sammy, this is her, and I say untuh you she is a dandy! Moreover I have tried her out! I have blew over Tourigny's henhouse; I have uprooted Dan Tate's windbreak, tooken the back door off of the schoolhouse, turned over the girls' toilet, three racks, six grain wagons. . . . In two hours did I cook her up; in two hours will I cook her down! (pp. 308–09)

British humour, in my experience, seems largely to depend on urbanity, irony, and especially on straight-faced, often elaborate presentation of the absurd as commonplace. I recall a weather report on the BBC one Wednesday night when the announcer, without the slightest change in tone, concluded his remarks by saying: "And toward midnight we shall be expecting scattered outbreaks of Thursday." The detailed film documentary on "spaghetti harvesting" in Italy is an example of the lengths to which the British will go, of a piece with Robertson Davies' Latin convocation address on behalf of Canadian bilingualism. In fact, it is quite likely that the secret of British survival in the face of repeated crises of one sort or another is that they do not take serious things seriously, but can either be or pretend to be deadly serious about the nonsensical and the ridiculous. The Flat Earth Society, episodes from the television program "Monty Python's Flying Circus" (*cf.* the American "Laugh-in") would serve as illustrations, as well as novels by Evelyn Waugh, Compton MacKenzie, or Kingsley Amis.

The British, it seems, are also more tolerant than North Americans of eccentrics and eccentricities, which perhaps explains why they do not find humour in oddballs and misfits so often as do humorists on this continent. I also suspect that the British, being less earnest and more cynical than North Americans in general have learned to be, are more adept at black humour.

Now anyone who has read Robertson Davies — *Leaven of Malice*, the play "Hunting Stewart", *The Table Talk of Samuel Marchbanks*, for instance — will recognize that he is much closer to Shaw and Amis than to Twain and Mitchell. Obviously Davies relies on urbanity, irony, and straight-faced presentation of the nonsensical rather than on comic diction, incongruity, naiveness, or exaggeration. In other words, his work is more in the British tradition of humour than in the North American, and that is why it gives the impression of being divorced from the general texture of those literary works most commonly regarded as reflecting the social values of Canada. Until, that is, Robertson Davies wrote *Fifth Business*.

It is almost as if Davies stopped taking dictation from an intellect imbued with the cream of English letters and began to write from his own feelings and experience of life, Canadian life. *Fifth Business* is a powerful book, rich in meaning and insight, and highly relevant to current thematic developments in Canadian fiction.

Written as a first-person narrative, *Fifth Business* is another offshoot of the ancient monologue form which has established itself so firmly in the Canadian consciousness. It is an *apologia pro vita sua* in the shape of a letter from a retired schoolmaster, Dunstan Ramsay, to the current headmaster of the school, a letter precipitated by a shallow and condescending tribute published in the school's journal. In many respects, however, Davies' *Fifth Business* may also be regarded as an *apologia pro patria sua* — an accounting for the Canadian nation.

The narrative is well-structured and captivatingly suspenseful. A seemingly trivial occurrence — Percy Boyd Staunton throwing a snowball at Dunstan (then called Dunstable) and inadvertently hitting Mary Dempster, the pregnant wife of the Baptist preacher — conditions the whole lives of Dunstan, Mary, and her son Paul, and eventually the death of "Boy" Staunton. The shock of being hit puts Mary into trauma and causes her to give birth prematurely, supplying at the same time the townspeople with a convenient explanation for Mary's behaviour unbecoming a minister's wife, both before and after the snowball.

The first part of *Fifth Business* is an inventory of small-town Canadian values in the era of the Old Order, when the Calvinist rationale still held full sway. Deptford is undoubtedly Davies' birthplace of Thamesville, Ontario, but it is typical of towns across the nation early in the twentieth century. It could be Sinclair Ross's Horizon or André Langevin's Macklin, or the towns in the novels of W. O. Mitchell and Jean Simard. As Ramsay describes it, while the "village contained much of what humanity has to show, it did not contain everything, and one of the things it conspicuously lacked was an aesthetic sense; we were all too much the descendants of hard-bitten pioneers to wish for or encourage any such thing, and we gave hard names to qualities that, in more sophisticated society, might have had value" (pp. 23–4).

Mary Dempster, wife of the zealous, Bible-thumping Amasa Dempster, bears the brunt of both her husband's and the town's Puritan morality. In some ways Mary is like a low-keyed Madeleine (of Langevin's *Poussière sur la ville*). She is pretty, sensual, childlike, spontaneous, and "utterly unfit to be a preacher's wife". She has a soft voice and smiles a great deal, "and the least she could have done was to take a stronger line with those waving tendrils of hair that seemed so often to be escaping from a properly severe arrangement." But unlike Madeleine, she is not completely egocentric — rather she is gentle and compassionate, which proves to be her undoing. One Friday night she disappears, and when she is finally located by a search party, she is unequivocally in "the act of copulation" with a partly deaf tramp. When her husband asks for an explanation, "He was very civil, 'Masa," she calmly replies, "And he wanted it so badly."

The village sense of decency, to be sure, is outraged beyond recall. Even Dunstan's rather reasonable mother, who nursed Mary through the premature birth and was largely responsible for saving the baby's life, washes her hands of the fallen woman, who becomes the butt of cruel jokes for the rest of her life in Deptford. It is not so much Mary's adultery that offends the town's right-thinking people, although that is bad enough, but it is the way she did it, her attitude, her apparent view that she had merely responded to the needs of another human being and acted naturally. The town and 'Masa make damned sure that she never acts "naturally" again. Her husband feels compelled to resign his ministry, and he thereafter keeps his wife confined in a cottage, literally on a rope leash.

Dunstan, however, is attached to Mrs. Dempster and to her son, Paul (also ostracized by the town), and he continues to visit her despite his mother's contrary commands. And just as Mrs. Ramsay saved Paul, Mary Dempster saves Dunstan, although in quite a different manner. What Mary saves Dunstan from is the dull, prodding, guilt-ridden, self-effacing role of the typical Calvinist-Jansenist-conditioned character in Canadian fiction. Through her, indirectly, he discovers the mystery and magic of life and starts on the path toward becoming the new type of Canadian hero, the self-reliant, individualistic, independent person found in Sinclair Ross's *Sawbones Memorial*, Adele Wiseman's *Crackpot*, and André Langevin's *Une Chaîne dans le parc*, and who is the subject of the first essay in this volume. Robertson Davies' character Dunstan Ramsay thus represents a remarkable and profound transition in Canadian values, for the observations of seasoned and perceptive writers such as Davies, Ross, Wiseman, and Langevin, among others, would not coincide without reflecting a phenomenon of Canadian society itself. Similar instances of groups of authors reacting at much the same time to a cultural transformation, long before people in general understand what is happening, can be seen in most national literatures.

The development of Dunstan Ramsay's character in *Fifth Business* provides an illuminating case history of how the Canadian phenomenon came about. As a boy, Ramsay has all the familiar traits of the old national hero. Because his ducking out of the way led to

Mary Dempster being hit by the snowball, he acquires a guilt complex: "I do not want to make foolish and sentimental claims for the suffering of a child. But even now I hesitate to recall some of the nights when I feared to go to sleep and prayed till I sweated that God would forgive me my mountainous crime" (p. 21). One thinks of the multitude of miserable children in Canadian literature, of the dirty-hands episode in *Who Has Seen the Wind*, or of Christian in Ducharme's *L'Avalée des avalés*, who torments himself because in reaction to taunts he looked at his beautiful cousin Mingrélie with her dress off. As Dunstan goes on to explain: "I was a Presbyterian child and I knew a good deal about damnation. . . . I was of the damned." Since "sins of the flesh" supposedly underscored man's carnal, unredeemed nature, the tendency was to magnify their presumed enormity, often out of proportion it would seem. In Quebec it used to be said that morality was found between the belly-button and the knee. "In my childhood," recalls Dunstan Ramsay, "the common attitude toward matters of sex was enough to make a hell of adolescence for any boy who was, like myself, deeply serious and mistrustful of whatever seemed pleasurable in life" (p. 22).

Davies' protagonist eventually masters his complex of guilt, but not until he is in his thirties. By then he has been through the First World War, lost a leg, and won the Victoria Cross. And Mary Dempster, whose son ran away from home as a small boy and whose husband died, has been living with an aunt in another town. Not long after Dunstan finds Mary (who is now really suffering from mental illness), the aunt dies:

> The next day I made inquiries as to how I could be appointed the guardian of Mary Dempster and found that it was not a very complicated process but would take time. I experienced a remarkable rising of my spirits, which I can only attribute to the relief of guilt. As a child I had felt oppressively responsible for her, but I had thought all that was dissipated in the war. Was not a leg full and fair payment for an evil action? This was primitive thinking, and I had no trouble dismissing it — so it seemed. But the guilt had only been thrust away, or thrust down out of sight, for here it was again, in full strength, clamouring to be atoned for, now that the opportunity offered itself. (p. 144)

Dunstan thus takes advantage of the opportunity to expiate his guilt with regard to Mary, but actually he is also paying her a more important debt, for the Baptist minister's wife has represented far greater things to him than a childhood mishap. It is in this respect, incidentally, that two Canadian books which could hardly be more contrasting in tone, style, technique, subject matter, atmosphere, and plot — *Fifth Business* and Leonard Cohen's *Beautiful Losers* — draw remarkably close together. In Cohen's novel the Iroquois saint Kateri Tekakwitha is symbolic of the capacity for mystery and faith, miracles and magic if you will, for which the narrator desperately yearns. One cannot imagine Robertson Davies articulating this yearning in quite the same phrases that Leonard Cohen uses to arrest the attention, but nevertheless Mary Dempster becomes for Dunstan exactly what Kateri was for Cohen's protagonist.

A part-time job looking after Deptford's small library is what sparks Dunstan's interest in magic and miracles. He used to take Paul Dempster there and read to him from *A Child's Book of Saints* and various books on the art of magic (the reason that Paul later becomes a renowned magician). But this spark would hardly have been sufficient to offset the hard-headed, no-nonsense, Puritan atmosphere in which Dunstan was raised. The turning point for him is when he is sitting alone with his severely sick brother, Willie, and the brother dies before his eyes — at least there is no evidence of breathing or pulse. In panic Dunstan rushes to the Dempster home, cuts the rope, and brings Mary:

> What I do remember was getting back to Willie's room . . . and finding him just as I had left him, white and cold and stiff. Mrs. Dempster looked at him solemnly but not sadly, then she knelt by the bed and took his hands in hers and prayed. I had no way of knowing how long she prayed, but it was less than ten minutes. I could not pray and did not kneel. I gaped — and hoped.
>   After a while she raised her head and called him. "Willie," said she in a low, infinitely kind, and indeed almost in a cheerful tone. Again, "Willie." I hoped till I ached. She shook his hands gently, as if rousing a sleeper. "Willie."
>   Willie sighed and moved his legs a little. I fainted. (p. 54)

From that day on, Dunstan Ramsay knows that there is more to life than what can be scientifically demonstrated, and that faith can mean strength and beauty as well as dreary dogma. An experience in the war, when he is lying gravely wounded and a flare lights up a statue of the Madonna in the wreckage of a church, confirms his belief — the face of the Virgin is Mary Dempster's face.

This is not to say, incidentally, that Ramsay becomes a raving or dreamy-eyed mystic, or even especially religious. He does for a

while flirt with the notion of having Mary declared a saint — a third
seemingly miraculous occurrence, as Dunstan later discovers, is that
Mary's gentle accommodation of the tramp in long-ago Deptford
led to his complete rehabilitation — but various Roman Catholic
authorities explain that the process is complicated and the case
hardly convincing. Deptford's Father Reagan suggests that Mary is
a "fool-saint", a person "who seems to be full of holiness and loves
everybody and does every good act he can, but because he's a fool
it all comes to nothing — to worse than nothing, because it is virtue
tainted with madness, and you can't tell where it'll end up" (p. 125).
What Dunstan eventually realizes, however, is that it is not so much
whether actual miracles have occurred or not, but the capacity to
believe that they might have which is important. In other words, to
allow life the extra dimension of mystery and magic is to liberate the
spirit and imagination, which can be smothered and destroyed by
unmitigated reality. They can also be smothered by Calvinistic
doctrine, which stultifies faith by assigning it a strictly limited
function, thereby fossilizing the mysteries. As Liesl, the woman who
works the magician show with Paul and who becomes Dunstan's
close friend and bed-mate, tells him:

> I know Calvinism as well as you do. It is a cruel way of life, even if
> you forget the religion and call it ethics or decent behaviour or some-
> thing else that pushes God out of it. . . . Oh, this Christianity! Even
> when people swear they don't believe in it, the fifteen hundred years
> of Christianity that has made our world is in their bones, and they
> want to show they can be Christians without Christ. Those are the
> worst; they have the cruelty of doctrine without the poetic grace of
> myth. (p. 202)

Through Mary, then later with "moral" support from Liesl,
Dunstan Ramsay finds "the poetic grace of myth". In fact, he becomes
a published authority on hagiography and mythic history, and the
interest proves to be a life-sustaining force, providing incentive to
travel widely, meet people, and do work which will be appreciated.
An old Jesuit tells him, "You and I have looked too deeply into
miracles to dogmatize; you believe in them, and your belief has
coloured your life with beauty and goodness." Whereas Boy Staunton,
devoted to money, power, influence, and the Prince of Wales,
destroys those around him, including Dunstan's old flame Leola,
Ramsay is a positive, creative person, enriching the lives of others.

By the time of his middle years he has progressed from a frightened, indoctrinated boy to an independent, individualistic, and self-confident man. The very form of the novel — a letter of rebuttal for a trite "portrait of myself as a typical old schoolmaster doddering into retirement" — is in itself an illustration of this point.

It is important to note that Dunstan Ramsay's interest in myth does not mean that he wishes to escape contemporary reality. He is not, to use a marvelous phrase from Cohen's *Beautiful Losers*, "chasing miracles with a bag of power to salt their wild tails." But he does wish to escape, to use another of Cohen's phrases, "the Desert of the Possible". There is, for instance, the matter of the two biographies, the fictional one which Ramsay ghostwrites for Paul Dempster (now called Magnus Eisengrim) and the one which he does not wish to write about the life of Boy Staunton. His unwillingness with regard to the latter is because he would have to whitewash the facts in order to make it acceptable. Now the question arises, how is it that Dunstan can take "delight" in writing one fake "life", yet have his sense of honesty rebel at the prospect of the other? The explanation, to my mind, is that in Staunton's case Dunstan is being asked to falsify and distort the truth, while in Paul's case he can, as it were, create myth to reveal the truth, a deeper truth, the psychological truth of Mary Dempster's premature son, whose childhood was made miserable by the town of Deptford, who travelled with carnivals and circuses around the world, and who eventually made himself into a renowned magician. I do not doubt that most autobiographies contain a certain amount of the same kind of myth, impressions of facts rather than the bare facts themselves, half-truths and untruths which nevertheless convey a more profound psychological truth. Even Frederick Philip Grove's discredited autobiography, *In Search of Myself*, reveals a great deal more about the man than all the "true" facts of Felix Paul Greve's life so-far researched. There is, therefore, no inconsistency about Dunstan Ramsay's willingness to write the "life" of Paul Dempster and unwillingness to do the same for Percy Boyd Staunton, the facts of whose life and the circumstances of whose death he knows more intimately than anyone else.

What Ramsay does not know intimately until late in life, until after he meets Liesl, is himself. It is she who suggests that he is "Fifth Business", an opera term the definition of which Davies supplies on a foreleaf to the novel:

Those roles which, being neither those of Hero nor Heroine, Confidante nor Villain, but which were nonetheless essential to bring about the Recognition or the dénouement, were called the Fifth Business in drama and opera companies organized according to the old style; the player who acted these parts was often referred to as Fifth Business.

We have already remarked how Ramsay's character development parallels changes taking place in Canadian society and reflected in the work of a number of prominent novelists, and the emphasis on myth in *Fifth Business* serves to accentuate the felt absence of positive myths in Canada. Dunstan Ramsay's identity problem also has much in common with that of the nation itself. For most of his life, Dunstan has played a low-keyed role, knowing who he was not, but not at all certain who or what he was supposed to be. Through Liesl, who tells him he is "just like a little boy", he comes to recognize that he has in fact been Fifth Business — "the one who knows the secret of the hero's birth," she explains, "or comes to the assistance of the heroine when she thinks all is lost, or keeps the hermitess in her cell, or may even be the cause of somebody's death if that is part of the plot." Dunstan fits all of these conditions, and eventually he admits to himself that he fills the role — "Fifth Business insisted on being heard again," he writes of himself at the fateful meeting between Paul and Boy at the end of the novel.

Dunstan's admission, however, should not be construed as defeatist or self-effacing; rather it is an honest acceptance of truth. According to the circumstances of his life, Dunstan Ramsay *is* Fifth Business, just as Canada in the arena of world powers cannot be considered otherwise. Nor is it necessarily advantageous to be otherwise. As Liesl once again points out: "It is not spectacular, but it is a good line of work, I can tell you, and those who play it sometimes have a career that outlasts the golden voices."

Another significant point to take into account is that the role of Fifth Business is defined in terms of one's relationship to others. It need not affect one's relationship to oneself — personal development and self-esteem. In accepting the truth, Dunstan gains new personal freedom for he acquires greater understanding of himself. He is urged by both Liesl and Padre Blazon, the aged Jesuit who befriended him, to make his life even fuller, to explore his personal devil, and perhaps also to get to know "his father, the Old Devil" — in other words, to stop denying the darker sides of his character, the shadows he knows so much about regarding the lives of saints. "The

Devil knows corners of us all of which Christ Himself is ignorant," says Padre Blazon. "Indeed, I am sure Christ learned a great deal that was salutary about Himself when He met the Devil in the wilderness" (p. 222).

Here again there is a marked parallel between *Fifth Business* and current tendencies in Canada. We have already noted the blossoming spirit of national independence and self-esteem, signalled in literature by the emergence of the new Canadian hero. There is also abroad a new spirit of inquiry, a desire to probe and to know the darker aspects of the Canadian totality. Exposés of racist immigration policy, ill-treatment of native peoples (including virtual annihilation of the Beothuks of Newfoundland), prejudices against blacks, Orientals, East Europeans, government stupidities, mismanagement of companies and unions, crimes of every sort — examples abound. Economists, social and political scientists, historians, journalists, television and radio scriptwriters — they're all at it. Even entertainers such as Quebec's popular Yvon Deschamps mix humour with bitter satire against the more unsavoury of ingrained Canadian attitudes. The stones are being turned over and the closets opened, and what comes to light is not always pleasant. But in the long run the effect will undoubtedly be, to borrow from Padre Blazon, "salutary".

Whatever the case, to return to the original contention of this analysis, Robertson Davies' *Fifth Business* is certainly relevant to this country's social evolution, and especially to current trends in the reshaping of values. It is, moreover, an optimistic, positive novel. Protagonist Dunstan Ramsay lives a difficult life, but he does not submit to the smothering of his human desire to seek deeper truths, and he finds within himself the imaginative capacity to avoid drab survival or self-destruction. Considering the parallels between Davies' hero and Canadian society, perhaps it is not unreasonable to expect that when enough Canadians are satisfied that they know the truth about themselves, we will at last be ready for "the poetic grace of myth".

5.
The Mainstream

Along with a number of other activities in Canada, literary criticism
has picked up a great deal of momentum in the last decade. Like the
St. Lawrence River it has deepened and broadened as it moved
along, and to a large extent it also has divided in two at the Island
of Montreal. In view of the mighty St. Lawrence's present state of
pollution, however, it would perhaps be injudicious to pursue the
analogy.

But it can be said with reasonable confidence that the steady
increase in the volume, variety, and contentiousness of Canadian
literary criticism is having and will continue to have a beneficial
effect on creative writing in this country. I imagine that there is
nothing more debilitating for a writer than to be ignored, to be
working in a vacuum as it were. Frederick Grove comes once again
to mind. Albert Laberge is another example.

Despite the recent increase in the volume of literary criticism,
however, several major problems remain to be resolved. They are
basic problems which glare like a hole in a girl's stocking or a pair
of mismatched socks, but they can also be covered up and ignored.
They would seem to invite attention, and then again they do not.
For they are often charged with emotional overtones. There is the
question, for instance, of who precisely is a Canadian author.
Anthologies and literary histories, to say the least, have tended to be
gloriously free of discrimination, grabbing all that could possibly be
grabbed. One wonders, indeed, how Jacques Maritain, Wyndham
Lewis, Willa Cather, and Ernest Hemingway, all of whom lived for
a time in Canada, escaped the conscription, not to mention Alexis
de Tocqueville, Charles Dickens, and Henry David Thoreau. Perhaps they escaped because their remarks about the True North
were often in a somewhat unappreciative vein.

But what about Frances Brooke, Louis Hémon, Brian Moore,
Malcolm Lowry, Arthur Hailey, Georges Bugnet, Robert Goulet (the
writer, not the actor), Jack Ludwig, even Leonard Cohen, Mordecai
Richler, François Hertel, and Marie-Claire Blais? Does citizenship
matter? Does it matter whether a writer came to this country after

growing up elsewhere, or went elsewhere after growing up here?
If one takes the view that where a person was born and grew up is
the determining factor, then the first six of the above dozen authors
must be disqualified as Canadian. If one takes the opposite view,
then at least four of the second six would have to go, and people like
A. J. M. Smith and Robert Kroetsch would have to go with them.
Or can we have it both ways? Are the pickings so slim that we cannot
afford to be fussy? Do we really have to stick national labels on
creative writers at all?

On the one hand, I am not especially concerned about national
labels, or at least about the application of national labels. As I have
suggested, it can be a tricky business, highly emotional as in the
case of certain Quebec poets who refuse to be called *poètes
canadiens* and insist on being *poètes québécois*. On the other hand,
it seems to me that in a relatively young country like Canada, with
its various complexes and crucial problems of national pride and
identity, it is necessary to seek definitions. To imagine that Canadian
criticism can become an organized scholarly discipline and attain
any degree of sophistication without defining its basic subject matter
is surely an example of disorganized and very unscholarly thinking.
Some critics and budding authors have attempted to avoid the issue
by proclaiming that a writer's universality is more important than
his "Canadianness". Of course it is. In the long run. But one must
keep in mind that an author does not become truly "international" by
virtue of intent, but by virtue of merit — by creating a vision which
transcends rather than disregards a particular national or regional
consciousness. Consider for a moment some of the more famous of
internationally recognized authors — Shakespeare, Molière, Burns,
Flaubert, Tolstoy, Dostoievski, Joyce, Twain, or Faulkner. It is not
without significance that these men were all strongly associated with
unmistakable national or even regional consciousness. It may not,
therefore, be entirely idle to speculate that the Canadian writer
most likely to achieve a lasting international reputation will be one
who at the same time is most obviously and thoroughly Canadian.

At the risk of infuriating the faithful of various camps, then, I am
going to explore the question of who is a Canadian writer, limiting
myself, of course, to those cases where there may be some measure
of doubt. Furthermore, I am going to present some observations
on the related question of the "mainstream" of Canadian literature,
a question I have already touched upon in a previous essay.[14]

The first problem, that of identifying the Canadian writers, may not be as mystifying as it seems. All writers produce their works from within a certain sphere of consciousness. Unless one subscribes to the notion of spirits from the great beyond guiding the pens of the entranced, then one must presume that a writer can express only what is within his awareness, however vague this awareness might be and whatever unforeseen or unrealized implications the writing might turn out to have. Consequently, the work of every writer must perforce be informed by the sphere or range of his consciousness, which in turn is the product of what might be called cultural conditioning. People think, feel, act, react, and express themselves in certain ways because of cultural conditioning and how this conditioning has shaped their hereditary potentials. Outside of complete brainwashing, this conditioning, the united effects of acquired knowledge and the experience of living in particular places, with particular people, and speaking a particular language at a particular time in history, is impossible to escape. When the biblical Joseph, after so many years in Egypt, overheard his unwitting brothers speak to each other in Hebrew, it is said that he turned and wept. James Sutherland, in his *Oxford Book of English Talk*, begins with a passage which seems to be in a strange and obscure tongue; he then goes on to explain that the passage is in the Aberdonian Scottish dialect which he spoke as a child, and that unintelligible as it may be to other people, it is soft music to his ears. Cultural conditioning makes the man. Although it is possible for this conditioning to be multilateral, for a person to be conditioned by more than one culture. Usually, however, there is a dominant influence, or at least one influence which eventually gains dominance, either consciously or unconsciously.

So far as the different levels of culture are concerned, the widening circle which begins with the cradle and, if unimpeded, progresses steadily through family, friends, community, nation, race, and mankind, most mature human beings live with the different levels simultaneously and without concern. The inner ripples, however being the earliest influences, are generally characterized by the greatest emotional involvement. The problem with Christ's two basic commandments, as Yvon Deschamps effectively intimates in his monologue "Le p'tit Jésus", is that few people, if any, seem capable of truly loving an abstract divinity or the whole human race.

Now in pinning a national label on a writer, I would suggest that the determining factor is not where he was brought up or where he has chosen to live, but rather the sphere of consciousness in which he has created his works, the result of his total cultural conditioning and especially of the dominant influences. Who would question that Ernest Hemingway was an American writer, despite the years he spent outside the United States? Or the Lachine-born Saul Bellow? Or James Baldwin? Or Richard Wright? Or Jack Kerouac, who finally turned an eye to Quebec in search of his "roots"? In the great majority of cases, the dominant influence is manifest, and there is no problem of identification. In other cases, rare but often important, two or more influences appear to be of equal strength, and the critic is obliged to create special categories. I am thinking of T. S. Eliot, Henry James, Samuel Beckett, and Karl Marx.

It is, of course, easier to determine the dominant cultural feature of a writer's sphere of consciousness after he is dead than to attempt to do so while he is still writing. Alive, he may yet shift one way or another. But I see no harm in making an informed inference, subject to adjustment in the light of possible further development. With regard to the dozen authors mentioned at the beginning of this essay, application of the dominant-influence sphere-of-consciousness criterion produces interesting conclusions. Of the six writers raised outside Canada — Brooke, Lowry, Hémon, Hailey, Moore, and Bugnet — only Hémon and Bugnet qualify to be considered authentic Canadian writers.

Brief as his stay was, brought to a tragic end by an accident in 1913, Louis Hémon, judging from his *Maria Chapdelaine*, became immersed in a distinctly Canadian sphere of consciousness. There are a number of reasons why this immersion should have taken place. Although born and raised in France, Hémon was hardly a typical Frenchman. He was from Brittany, an area which has resisted to some extent the formidable assimilative power of French culture and from which, incidentally, came some of the ancestors of French Canadians. Moreover, Hémon was apparently repelled by the French civilization which surrounded him. He went to England, stayed eight years, and wrote a sports story called "Battling Malone", among other things, but then decided that English civilization was just as decadent as that on the continent. Seeking the primitive and natural in human beings, he evidently found what he was looking for in rural Quebec. The cultural atmosphere was compatible, and he was able to lose himself in it, to become attuned to its nuances and subtleties. Louis Hémon did not write more novels, and had he done so, perhaps he might have revealed that his cultural immersion in Quebec was only temporary. But on the basis of the sphere of consciousness which produced *Maria Chapdelaine*, a classic so well known that it requires no commentary here, it is appropriate to consider Louis Hémon as a Canadian author.

Georges Bugnet ought to be likewise considered. From a town in east central France, at the age of twenty-six, he settled in a wilderness area of Alberta shortly after the turn of the century. In his forties, during the periods of winter isolation, he began to write books. His novels *Nipsya*, the story of an Irish-Cree halfbreed, and *La Forêt*, an impressive study of the effects upon the human soul of a constant struggle against the vast Canadian bushland, reveal that Bugnet's sphere of consciousness became dominantly conditioned by his life here. One may not agree with the theme of *Nipsya*, that Christian resignation is the only hope for the Cree Indians, but there can be no doubt about Bugnet's acquired sensitivity to the peculiarities of the people, including Indian, métis, and white, and to the particularities of the physical geography and climate of his adopted country. In this respect he closely resembles that other writer of the West, Frederick Philip Grove.

By contrast, the works of Frances Brooke, Brian Moore, Malcolm Lowry, and Arthur Hailey do not reflect any significant or extended immersion in a Canadian sphere of consciousness. Mrs. Brooke, who spent five years in this country when her husband was chaplain to the Quebec garrison, was by no stretch of the imagination culturally influenced in any way except that her conviction of the superiority of the English race, upper-class division, was confirmed. Of course, at the time when she was here, 1763–68, there was hardly anything to be culturally influenced by in any case. Why, then, should she be referred to as the first Canadian novelist, or her *History of Emily Montague* be called the first Canadian novel in English? She would undoubtedly have been shocked to the tips of her manicured fingernails if anyone had suggested to her that she was anything other than a purebred English writer.

Brian Moore, on the other hand, seems to have had no particular objection to being called Canadian. In an interview quoted by Hallvard Dahlie in his book *Brian Moore*, Moore states:

> Then when it might have seemed that someone in Ireland might have started writing about me, it was announced that I was living in Canada and was really a Canadian who was pretending to write Irish novels. I embraced the Canadians with both arms and became a Canadian

citizen and announced to everyone that I was a Canadian writer, whereupon I spent my life being told by Canadians that I'm not really Canadian. (p. 2)

One can sympathize with Moore; although with his proven and acknowledged talent as a writer, he is hardly in need of anyone's sympathy. I can distinctly recall, however, another of his published remarks, in *Le Devoir* some years ago, where he states that he could never think as a Canadian nor fit into the pattern of Canadian literature. Actually, George Woodcock's categorization of Moore as one of those "splendid birds of passage" appears to sum up the situation precisely. Moore did live in Montreal for a time, and he chose that city for the setting of his entertaining and charming novel *The Luck of Ginger Coffey*. But a setting does not mean a sphere of consciousness, an inside awareness of subtle peculiarities. *Ginger Coffey* no more makes Brian Moore a Canadian writer than *For Whom the Bell Tolls* makes Hemingway Spanish. In evaluating the sphere of consciousness in which a book was created, characterization is obviously of far greater significance than setting or atmosphere. The question to be posed is: to what extent does the author develop characters who are recognizably Canadian in more than name? There are no such characters in Moore's *Ginger Coffey*. The protagonist is a whimsical, impractical Irish immigrant, and the one "Canadian" who is developed to any extent is Grosvenor, who remains a vague shell to the end and whose major attribute is that he has an eye for Ginger's pretty wife. Another of Moore's novels, *I Am Mary Dunne*, has a protagonist who is nominally a Nova Scotian, but the novel, set in New York, is concerned with the problems of being a woman rather than a Nova Scotian. *The Revolution Script*, rushed out after the October Crisis, is of course essentially band-wagon reportage, and Moore's latest work is set in California, where he now lives. Brian Moore is an excellent writer, and no doubt history will decide whether he ends up with any kind of national label. On the basis of his novels to date, however, it makes absolutely no sense to call him a Canadian author, Governor General's Award notwith-standing.

Arthur Hailey's situation is much like that of Moore. He was born and educated in Britain, came to Canada for a time, then went to the United States, and he is now living, I believe, somewhere in the Caribbean, collecting seven-figure royalties, which in itself is definitely un-Canadian. He too has used a Canadian setting for his political novel *In High Places*, but he has since moved on to higher places.

Malcolm Lowry? What can one say about Malcolm Lowry? I would dearly love to be able to consider Lowry a Canadian writer. But on what grounds? He lived a few years on the West Coast, then returned to England. He used a Canadian setting for the novella "The Forest Path to the Spring". Regarding the posthumously published *October Ferry to Gabriola*, George Woodcock feels that "it does become evident that he reacted with deep emotion and commitment to his Canadian environment." Yet in his masterpiece *Under the Volcano*, Lowry reacts with at least equal emotion to the Mexican environment. So far as sphere of consciousness is concerned, Lowry seems to be in a kind of no-man's land, or perhaps every-man's land would be more exact. Further research and deeper understanding of Malcolm Lowry's art may modify this view, but for the moment I see nothing significantly Canadian about his sphere of consciousness. And just in case there is doubt in anyone's mind, I should make clear at this point that whether or not an author can be considered Canadian has no connection whatsoever with the literary merit of his work.

There is, accordingly, no reasonable justification for Canadian literature to claim Brooke, Hailey, Moore, or Lowry, all of whom were culturally conditioned elsewhere and whose spheres of consciousness were not noticeably affected by their sojourns in Canada. Swinging over to those writers who were born and raised in Canada, then moved away either permanently or for an extended period, the same argument which excludes four of the six foreign-born authors can be used to preserve Canadian claim to at least five of the second half-dozen: Leonard Cohen, François Hertel, Mordecai Richler, Marie-Claire Blais, and Robert Goulet. Each of these writers may in the course of time become assimilated into another sphere of consciousness, but so far, judging from their major works, the Canadian cultural factor is still manifestly dominant. Goulet has not produced much to go on of late, but *The Violent Season* is as Canadian as a book can be, set in a lumber camp and bitterly describing the influence of the church in French Canada. Hertel's and Richler's principal writings are also distilled from a Canadian awareness, even if the same cannot be said for each man's total production to date. Richler, of course, is a thorough professional who leans toward the trendy (accounting for his weakest work, such as *Cocksure* and *St. Urban's Horseman*) and who tries to rise above the Canadian

association, but one could hardly imagine Mordecai Richler without
Canada to bitch about, especially now that he is living here again.

Jack Ludwig, on the other hand, makes an interesting contrast
with the other two Jewish-Canadian-born authors, Richler and
Leonard Cohen. All three are naturally more or less concerned with
the Jew in North America, but Cohen's *Favourite Game* and
Beautiful Losers and Richler's *Son of a Smaller Hero* and *Apprenticeship of Duddy Kravitz*, all four novels set in Montreal, are distinctly
Canadian. They are, in fact, when compared with Jack Ludwig's
Confusions or the works of Jewish-American writers such as Philip
Roth and J. D. Salinger, much more Canadian than they are Jewish.
As critics have often pointed out, the novels of Cohen and Richler
listed above embody many of the characteristic themes of Canadian
literature — the land, the Old Order *versus* materialism, the profound
nothingness that results from a break with the established system,
the frantic search for replacement values. Ludwig's *Confusions*, in
striking contrast, is American through and through, from the comic
quasi-dedication to Richard Nixon, Tennessee Williams, Liberace,
J. Edgar Hoover, Mitch Miller, and other institutions of the United
States, to the settings in Ivy League New England and a small
college in California. The book is funny, and stylistically clever *à la
New Yorker*. It is part of a strong trend in contemporary American
fiction — the new novel of manners, distinguished from the former
variety by its complete sexual frankness and its poking beneath the
surface to expose the hidden quirks of the social animal. The theme
of *Confusions*, the individualist resisting pressures to conform, is
of course as archetypically American as Coca-Cola and Manifest
Destiny. The only recognizable feature of the one nominally "Canadian" character in the book, a Cree Indian who spouts Thoreau,
sexually services a good proportion of American womanhood, and
talks in the idiom of the mod graduate student, is that he dislikes
American beer. He has come a long way from Georges Bugnet's
Crees. There can be no question, therefore, that Jack Ludwig's
Confusions was created from a sphere of consciousness that is in any
respect Canadian.

Like Louis Hémon, Ludwig appears to have been able to become
effectively immersed in a new sphere of consciousness. He has taught
for years in the United States, and it would seem that his novel is
distilled exclusively from that experience. It is of interest perhaps
to note here that Ludwig is one of a considerable number of Canadians who have been attracted to teaching positions in the United

States. Some of these expatriates, A. J. M. Smith and Robert Kroetsch for example, seem to defy cultural assimilation, while others are drawn rapidly into the American sphere. In Ludwig's case, the extent to which he has been drawn into the sphere still remains to be seen. *Confusions* may eventually prove to be an isolated instance, for Ludwig's other fiction often relates to his Canadian consciousness. For the time being, however, Jack Ludwig remains a doubtful case so far as a national label is concerned.

To return to our original list of twelve writers, we must conclude that when the works of each are examined in light of the sphere-of-consciousness criterion, only seven remain as authentically Canadian, with an eighth as a possibility.

I have not, of course, exhausted the list of immigrant or expatriate writers whose inclusion in anthologies and histories of Canadian literature leaves room for doubt. Patrick Anderson, Arthur Stringer, Marie Le Franc, Maurice Constantin-Weyer, David Walker, Robert Fontaine, Norman Levine, Thomas Costain, Lionel Shapiro, Mavis Gallant, Michael Sheldon, and Gerald Taaffe are some of the other names which come to mind. But an exhaustive investigation is not my intention; rather I want to suggest and to illustrate a criterion which is possibly more sound and sensitive than whatever has operated in the past. This criterion, based upon analysis of an author's sphere of consciousness as revealed in his published works, is certainly more reliable than the circumstantial evidence of birth-place, citizenship, settings of books, or sojourns in Canada.

I might add, incidentally, that the phenomenon of certain Quebec writers not wishing to be called *canadien* is more psychological and political than literary. The very statement presupposes a sphere of consciousness which is acutely Canadian, at least as long as Quebec remains a part of Canada. Paradoxically, there is also something peculiarly Canadian about the wish not to be considered simply Canadian in the political sense, for as I pointed out earlier in the discussion of multi-cultural nationalism, political nationalism has never been strong in this country. Moreover, so far as the terms *canadien français* and *québécois* are concerned, the latter has now taken on special overtones. It symbolizes the new, dynamic, progressive Quebecker, as opposed to the backward, inferiority-complex-ridden *canadien français*. And overtones attached to a name, however fleeting they may be, can be tremendously important to the people involved, as we know from the shift through coloured, negro, black, and Afro-American in the United States.

Now the concept of a writer's sphere of consciousness not only serves for general identification purposes; it also has bearing on what I believe to be the emerging mainstream of Canadian literature. Within Canada itself, because of the vastness of the land and the diversification of cultural influences, there are numerous possible spheres of consciousness. Actually, each individual's sphere will be at least slightly different from another's, but general transcendent patterns can be discerned. In Canadian literature, these general patterns are often associated with geographical area — Toronto, Winnipeg, Vancouver, Quebec City, rural Quebec, rural Ontario, the Atlantic seaboard, the small town, the prairies, the foothills of the Rockies, English Montreal, French Montreal, Jewish Montreal. Some of the general spheres in Canada are very similar to those in the United States, the small town and the prairies for instance. In addition, more often than not American writers have created influential works from within these spheres, making it a challenge for Canadians to produce something strikingly original or distinctive. Nevertheless, some of our writers — Sinclair Ross, Margaret Laurence, and W. O. Mitchell, for example — have now clearly proven themselves equal to the challenge, and their method has been to focus thematically on the peculiar psychological conditioning of Canadians discussed in the essay "The New Hero".

On the other hand, a sphere of consciousness which is uniquely Canadian does exist in this country, and from within this sphere the mainstream of Canadian literature is rapidly emerging.

The distinguishing feature of the sphere of consciousness which governs the mainstream of Canadian literature is, understandably enough, the same feature which principally distinguishes the Canadian nation — the co-existence in this country of two major ethnic or language groups. There are several other side-streams, some conditioned by attitudes which derive from the Calvinist and Jansenist traditions, such as the phenomenon of the *prêtre manqué* which has recurred so often in works of both language groups; a good amount of Quebec literature is floating along in these Canadian side-streams, just as much Canadian writing in both French and English is in various tributaries of British, French, and American literature. Lately, however, the mainstream has been gathering force.

May I repeat once again that the mainstream of Canadian literature has nothing to do with literary merit; it is a matter of sphere of consciousness, an author's awareness of and sensitivity to fundamental aspects of both major language groups in Canada, and of the inter-relationships between these two groups. Now I know that the idea of a mainstream bothers some writers and critics, who seem to presume that it is akin to the Order of Canada or whatever it is that the government put into operation to celebrate the centennial, inanely proclaiming certain writers first-class, others second-class, and the rest beneath classification. In fact, however, the mainstream concept is a thematic identification and not a value judgment. There is no need for a writer to be in the mainstream in order to achieve literary quality, as indeed many of the Canadian writers of merit are not. Adele Wiseman, Sinclair Ross, Robertson Davies, W. O. Mitchell, Louis Hémon, Alice Munro, Morley Callaghan, and Stephen Leacock are obvious examples. But that there must be a mainstream, however, is to me a matter of syllogistic logic, for as I will further elaborate below, in order to have a Canadian literature it is necessary to have a Canadian nation, and the survival of the Canadian nation presupposes a *modus vivendi* between the nation's two major language groups. Moreover, the mainstream awareness and sensitivity I am talking about is nothing unusual in national literatures. As critics in the United States have often pointed out, seminal American writers — Melville, Twain, Cooper, Faulkner — accurately sensed that the survival of their nation depended upon Americans of different races finding a mutually acceptable *modus vivendi*.

At one time, only a few years ago in fact, Hugh MacLennan appeared almost the only modern, major creative writer in Canada who was moving with the mainstream current. Certain authors of the past — political writers, commentators, journalists — had been swept up, but not major creative writers. A few writers in each language group, of course, had indicated a superficial awareness of the other, resulting in the stereotyped anglophones in such books as Jean Simard's *Les Sentiers de la nuit* or Lionel Groulx's *L'Appel de la race*, and stereotyped French Canadians in the works of Ralph Connor, Hugh Garner, Morley Callaghan, or Ellis Portal. But in recent years, several Canadian authors have been drawn into the mainstream, have developed much more than a superficial awareness. Hugh Hood, both in his novels and his stories, is one example. James Bacque in the novel *Big Lonely*, Leonard Cohen in *Beautiful Losers*, Ralph Gustafson in his recent poetry, Dave Godfrey both explicitly and symbolically, Margaret Atwood in *Survival*, D. G. Jones in *Butterfly on Rock* and his latest poems, Louis Dudek, Frank Scott, and John Glassco, the last three heightening an awareness they have always had, George Woodcock, Philip Stratford, who is also a skilled translator, Fred Cogswell, Christina Roberts, Max Dorsinville, Clément Moisan, Antoine Sirois, even Al Purdy and George Ryga, are only some of the others. The recent wave of translations and the magazine *Ellipse* out of the Université de Sherbrooke, presenting contemporary anglophone and francophone Canadian writers in translation, are still other examples of literary activity governed by the sphere of consciousness which characterizes the mainstream of Canadian literature.

Among French-language Quebec writers, ironically enough, those who are the most nationalistic, who do not want to be called *canadiens*, are generally the very ones who are right in the middle of the Canadian mainstream. For clearly they have the most acute awareness of the anglophone presence in Canada, of *la mentalité anglo-saxonne* as it is often put. In contrast to so many Quebec writers of the past, who were in tributaries of French literature or in little Quebec side-streams of their own, contemporary authors such as Jacques Godbout, Hubert Aquin, Roch Carrier, Claude Jasmin, Gérard Bessette, to mention just a few, have waded to varying depths in the mainstream, exhibiting in their works an indisputable, even if sometimes subjectively painful, consciousness of the co-existence of two major ethnic groups in Canada. Compare, for instance, the spheres of consciousness of the above with those of St.-Denys Garneau, Albert Lozeau, or Emile Nelligan. Among the *chansonniers*, compare Gilles Vigneault with the more recent arrival Robert Charlebois.

Another irony is that the one phenomenon which has probably done more than anything else to get the mainstream of Canadian literature flowing, the stroke that finally burst the dam of isolation as it were, is the upsurge in Quebec separatism. It has had the effect of shattering the two solitudes and of tremendously increasing mutual awareness in the language groups of Canada; it has created the tension, turmoil, anxiety, soul-searching, and commitment which, unfortunate as the fact may be in terms of tranquil existence, are the stuff of great literature.

Quebec separatism, thus, has turned out to be a powerful motivating force in the emergence of the mainstream of Canadian literature. In a way, also, it has become a guarantee of the truth and legitimacy of the whole concept of a mainstream. For clearly, if enough English-speaking and French-speaking Canadians do not become engulfed in a sphere of consciousness embracing a mutual awareness and comprehension, then Canada as a nation is not likely to survive. Which means, of course, that the question of a mainstream of Canadian literature will become an exercise in redundancy. Conversely, if Canada does survive as a nation, it will mean that the mainstream sphere of consciousness has in fact prevailed, that enough representatives — there will always be those who through will or circumstances remain in their own cultural compartments — of the two major ethnic groups have actually developed a sufficiently effective awareness and comprehension of each other.

One should not underestimate the force and importance of this awareness, which does not mean love and kisses and a big happy family. Sociologists and ethnologists have of late been swinging around to the view that pluralist societies, those made up of several distinct and largely autonomous ethnic or cultural groups held together by a flexible and loose political superstructure, can survive and are indeed preferable to homogeneous national communities, the kinds of nations where one man can provoke 98 per cent of the citizens to stand up and shout "My country right or wrong". Sidney Mintz, for instance, in speaking of the Caribbean nations, makes a general observation which is peculiarly relevant to the present Canadian situation. He states that the view "[that] those societies with the greatest sense of national identity will also be those whose populations are most homogeneous in their values . . . is not supported by fact." He goes on to explain that "not the number of groups, but the extent to which they interpenetrate in the maintenance of communication and in the solution of national issues . . . [is] the critical factor. National identity can be built in part on the recognition of conflict as integrating, and does not require cultural homogeneity."[15]

Conflict (meaning the clash of ideas), therefore, and the lack of cultural homogeneity, two prominent characteristics of contemporary Canada, although considered vital shortcomings in the nineteenth-century concept of nationhood, may well turn out to be the very reverse in the twentieth century. But communication is the key, and communication between the segments of Canada, "interpenetration" if you will, is steadily increasing; if the mainstream of Canadian literature continues to gather force, it will increase even more.

The essays in this volume have attempted to focus attention on a few of the crucial changes now occurring in Canadian society and being reflected in the mirror of Canadian literature. We are at the moment of serious re-evaluation, definition, purification, and consolidation — finding ourselves as it were. We have already conceived a new Canadian hero, and we are changing the image of ourselves in our minds. Cultural nationalism is in all parts of the nation resulting in a notable increase in all areas of literary activity. And this increase, happily, is coupled with a heightened awareness of that activity. Perhaps, like the great *Fleuve St-Laurent*, despite obstacles, rapids, shores in the United States, divisions, and pollution, we may yet find our way to the open sea.

Notes

[1] See *The Montreal Gazette* (Nov. 15, 1975), p. 8.

[2] *Second Image: Comparative Studies in Quebec/Canadian Literature* (New Press, 1971) traces in detail the parallel development of Canadian literature in English and French, including the many expressions of the Calvinist-Jansenist tradition.

[3] "Self-Conscious Canadians," *Canadian Literature*, 62 (Autumn, 1974), pp. 6–16.

[4] "Il pleure subitement, sans qu'il ait senti venir les larmes, mais de rage, contre elles, leur mise en scène, leur façon d'être vieilles et vivantes, de le traîner là comme s'il était coupable, lui-même, ou à la place d'un autre, et d'en faire une sainte quand elles ne peuvent parler de personne sans le dépecer vivant." (p. 247)

[5] "Et lui, il comprend qu'il y a la tribu de ceux qui refusent de se soumettre, comme tous les autres, à ce qu'on attend d'eux et qui a été décidé par il ne sait qui, une autre tribu, beaucoup plus nombreuse, portant veston et cravate, instruite et pas fière, qui, tous les jours, va travailler au même endroit, pendant vingt, trente ans, accorde la plus grande importance aux têtes tranchées de rois déguisées en têtes ordinaires sur des pièces de monnaie et n'a même pas un regard pour une bille qui peut teinter le soleil de couleurs si belles. ..." (p. 267)

[6] Quoted by Colin McGlashan in *The New Statesman* (July 28, 1972).

[7] See *Selections from Canadian Poets*, ed. Edward Hartley Dewart (Montreal: John Lovell, 1864).

[8]Interview in *The Montreal Gazette* (Dec. 2, 1972).

[9]"Le Monologue québécois," *Canadian Literature*, 58 (Autumn, 1973), p. 28.

[10]See "Here's A Whole New World For You," *Canadian Magazine* (December 9, 1972).

[11]From *Poésie acadienne — La Revue de l'Université de Moncton* (January 1972).

[12]"Il avait empoigné son Sten par la courroie, lui faisait faire un moulinet qui déchiqueta une branche d'arbre au-dessus de sa tête; il le rabattit dans la figure de son insulteur, qui tomba foudroyé. Lanthier dirigea vers son ventre le canon du Sten et pressa la détente jusqu'à ce que le chargeur fût vide. L'Allemand sursauta, et, pendant quelques instants, fut agité d'une convulsion hideuse. Puis son corps se tordit comme celui d'un ver et s'immobilisa finalement." (p. 143)

[13]In *Le Roman canadien-français, Archives des lettres canadiennes*, III (Montreal: Fides, 1964), pp. 338–39: "Jouirons-nous jamais, nous romanciers canadiens-français, de la même indépendance, du même sentiment de force linguistique? Il me semble que non. Que nous faudrait-il en effet? Rien de moins qu'une population, qu'une influence politique, culturelle et militaire comparables à celles de la France. (C'est le cas des Etats-Unis vis-à-vis l'Angleterre.) Jusque-là nous ne pouvons pas (nous ne pouvons pas même souhaiter) laisser évoluer notre langue "naturellement". Car ce serait vouloir remplacer une langue "universelle" par un dialecte."

[14]See "The Fourth Kind of Separatism" in *Second Image*.

[15]"Caribbean Nationhood in Anthropological Perspective," *Caribbean Integration* (1967), p. 153. Available in Bobbs-Merrill Reprint Series in Black Studies, BC-206.

Bibliography:

The editions listed are those which I have used in preparing this volume and my previous volume of related essays, *Second Image* (Toronto: General Publishing, 1975), and to which all page references in the text are made. Generally these editions are the most readily available. The abbreviation "NCL" is for the New Canadian Library Series of McClelland and Stewart Ltd., Toronto. See separate listing for translations.

PRIMARY SOURCES

Allister, William. *A Handful of Rice*. London: Secker & Warburg, 1961.

Aquin, Hubert. *Prochain épisode*. Montréal: Cercle du Livre de France, 1965.

———. *Trou de mémoire*. Montréal: Cercle du Livre de France, 1968.

———. *L'Antiphonaire*. Montréal: Cercle du Livre de France, 1969.

———. *Neige noire*. Montréal: Editions La Presse, 1974.

Archambault, Gilles. *Les Pins parasols*. Montréal: Editions Quinze, 1976.

Atwood, Margaret. *The Edible Woman*. Toronto: McClelland and Stewart, 1969.

———. *Surfacing*. Toronto: McClelland and Stewart, 1972.

Aubert de Gaspé, Philippe. *Les Anciens Canadiens*. Montréal: Fides, 1961.

Bacque, James. *Big Lonely*. Toronto: New Press, 1970.

———. *A Man of Talent*. Toronto: New Press, 1972.

Barbeau, Charles-Marius. *Le Rêve de Kamalmouk*. Montréal: Fides, 1948.

Beaulieu, Victor-Lévy. *Mémoires d'outre-tonneau*. Montréal: Editions Estérel, 1968.

———. *Les Grand-pères*. Montréal: Editions du Jour, 1971.

———. *Un Rêve québécois*. Montréal: Editions du Jour, 1972.

———. *Oh Miami Miami Miami*. Montréal: Editions du Jour, 1973.

Bell, Donald. *Saturday Night at the Bagel Factory*. Toronto: McClelland and Stewart, 1972.

Benoît, Jacques. *Jos Carbone*. Montréal: Editions du Jour, 1967.

Beresford-Howe, Constance. *The Book of Eve*. Toronto: Macmillan, 1973.

Bessette, Gérard. *La Bagarre*. Montréal: Cercle du Livre de France, 1958.

——. *Le Libraire*. Montréal: Cercle du Livre de France, 1960.

——. *Les Pédagogues*. Montréal: Cercle du Livre de France, 1961.

——. *L'Incubation*. Montréal: Librairie Déom, 1965.

Birney, Earle. *Turvey*. NCL 34, 1963.

Blais, Marie-Claire. *La Belle Bête*. Montréal: Cercle du Livre de France, 1958.

——. *Tête blanche*. Québec: Institut littéraire, 1960.

——. *Le Jour est noir*. Montréal: Editions du Jour, 1962.

——. *Une Saison dans la vie d'Emmanuel*. Montréal: Editions du Jour, 1965.

——. *L'Insoumise*. Montréal: Editions du Jour, 1966.

——. *David Sterne*. Montréal: Editions du Jour, 1967.

——. *Manuscrits de Pauline Archange*. Montréal: Editions du Jour, 1968.

——. *Le Loup*. Montréal: Editions du Jour, 1972.

——. *Un Joualonais sa joualonie*. Montréal: Editions du Jour, 1973.

Blaise, Clark. *A North American Education*. Toronto: Doubleday, 1973.

Blicker, Seymour. *Shmucks*. Toronto: McClelland and Stewart, 1972.

Bosco, Monique. *La Femme de Loth*. Montréal: HMH, 1970.

Boyle, Harry. *The Great Canadian Novel*. Toronto: Doubleday, 1972.

Brooke, Frances. *The History of Emily Montague*. NCL 27, 1961.

Buckler, Ernest. *The Mountain and the Valley*. NCL 23, 1961.

Buell, John. *The Pyx*. Toronto: Ambassador, 1959.

——. *Four Days*. New York: Farrar Straus & Cudahy, 1962.

——. *The Shrewesdale Exit*. Toronto: Doubleday, 1972.

Callaghan, Morley. *Such Is My Beloved*. Toronto: Macmillan, 1934. Also NCL 2, 1957.

——. *The Loved and the Lost*. Toronto: Macmillan, 1951.

——. *More Joy in Heaven*, NCL 17, 1960.

——. *A Passion in Rome*. Toronto: Macmillan, 1961.

——. *They Shall Inherit the Earth*. NCL 33, 1963.

——. *A Fine and Private Place.* Toronto: Macmillan, 1975.

Carrier, Roch. *La Guerre, yes sir!* Montréal: Editions du Jour, 1968.

——. *Floralie, où es-tu?* Montréal: Editions du Jour, 1969.

——. *Il est par là, le soleil.* Montréal: Editions du Jour, 1970.

——. *Le Deux-millième Étage.* Montréal: Editions du Jour, 1973.

Carroll, Jock. *The Shy Photographer.* New York: Stein & Day, 1964.

Charbonneau, Robert. *Ils posséderont la terre.* Montréal: L'Arbre, 1941.

Child, Philip. *The Village of Souls.* Toronto: Ryerson, 1948.

Choquette, Robert. *La Pension Leblanc.* Montréal: Editions du Mercure, 1927.

——. *Elise Velder.* Montréal: Fides, 1958.

Cloutier, Eugène. *Les Témoins.* Montréal: Cercle du Livre de France, 1953.

Cohen, Leonard. *The Favourite Game.* London: Secker & Warburg, 1963.

——. *Beautiful Losers.* Toronto: McClelland and Stewart, 1966.

Cohen, Matt. *Johnny Crackle Sings.* Toronto: McClelland and Stewart, 1971.

Conan, Laure (pseud. for Félicité Angers). *Angéline de Montbrun.* Montréal: Fides, 1967.

Connor, Ralph. *The Man from Glengarry.* NCL 14, 1960.

Cowasjee, Saros. *Goodbye to Elsa.* Toronto: New Press, 1974.

Davies, Robertson. *Tempest-tost.* Toronto: Clarke Irwin, 1950.

——. *Leaven of Malice.* Toronto: Clarke Irwin, 1954.

——. *A Mixture of Frailties.* Toronto: Macmillan, 1958.

——. *Fifth Business.* New York: Signet, 1971.

——. *The Manticore.* Toronto: Macmillan, 1972.

——. *World of Wonders.* Toronto: Macmillan, 1975.

Decotret, Claude. *Mourir en automne.* Montréal: L'Actuelle, 1971.

De la Roche, Mazo. *Delight.* NCL 21, 1961.

Deschamps, Yvon. *Monologues.* Montréal: Leméac, 1973.

Desmarchais, Rex. *La Chesnaie.* Montréal: L'Arbre, 1942.

Doutremont, Henri (pseud. for Georges Bugnet). *Nipsya.* Montréal: Garand, 1924.

Ducharme, Réjean. *L'Avalée des avalés.* Paris: Gallimard, 1966.

——. *Le Nez qui voque.* Paris: Gallimard, 1967.

——. *L'Océantume.* Paris: Gallimard, 1968.

——. *L'Hiver de force.* Paris: Gallimard, 1973.

Duncan, Sara Jeannette. *The Imperialist.* NCL 20, 1961.

Elie, Robert. *La Fin des songes.* Montréal: Beauchemin, 1950.

——. *Il suffit d'un jour.* Montréal: Beauchemin, 1957.

Engel, Marian. *The Honeyman Festival.* Toronto: Anansi, 1971.

——. *Bear.* Toronto: McClelland and Stewart, 1976.

Fennario, David (pseud. for David Wiper?). *Without a Parachute.* Toronto: McClelland and Stewart, 1974.

Ferron, Jacques. *Cotnoir.* Montréal: Editions d'Orphée, 1962.

——. *L'Amélanchier.* Montréal: Editions du Jour, 1970.

——. *Les Roses sauvages.* Montréal: Editions du Jour, 1971.

——. *Le Saint-Elias.* Montréal: Editions du Jour, 1972.

Fontaine, Robert. *The Happy Time.* New York: Dell, 1945.

France, Claire (pseud. for Claire Morin). *Les Enfants qui s'aiment.* Montréal: Beauchemin, 1956.

Fraser, Sylvia. *Pandora.* Toronto: McClelland and Stewart, 1972.

——. *The Candy Factory.* Toronto: McClelland and Stewart, 1974.

Garner, Hugh. *Storm Below.* Toronto: Ryerson, 1949.

——. *The Silence on the Shore.* Toronto: McClelland and Stewart, 1962.

——. *Cabbagetown.* Toronto: Ryerson, 1969.

——. *Violation of the Virgins.* Toronto: McGraw-Hill Ryerson, 1971.

——. *The Intruders.* Toronto: McGraw-Hill Ryerson, 1975.

Gérin-Lajoie, Antoine. *Jean Rivard.* Montréal: Beauchemin, 1953.

Girard, Rodolphe. *Marie Calumet.* Montréal: Editions Serge Brosseau, 1946.

Giroux, André. *Au delà des visages.* Montréal: Variétés, 1948.

——. *Le Gouffre a toujours soif.* Québec: Institut littéraire, 1953.

Godbout, Jacques. *L'Aquarium.* Paris: Seuil, 1962.

——. *Le Couteau sur la table.* Paris: Seuil, 1965.

——. *Salut Galarneau!* Paris: Seuil, 1967.

——. *D'Amour, P.Q.* Montréal: HMH, 1972.

Godfrey, Dave. *Death Goes Better with Coca Cola.* Toronto: Anansi, 1967.

——. *The New Ancestors.* Toronto: New Press, 1970.

Goulet, Robert. *The Violent Season.* New York: G. Braziller, 1961.

Graham, Angus. *Napoleon Tremblay.* London: R. Hale, 1939.

Graham, Gwethalyn. *Earth and High Heaven.* NCL 13, 1960.

Gravel, Pierre. *A perte de temps.* Toronto/Montreal: Anansi/Parti Pris, 1969.

Grignon, Claude-Henri. *Un Homme et son péché.* Montréal: Centre educatif et culturel, 1965.

Groulx, Lionel. *L'Appel de la race.* Montréal: Fides, 1962.

Grove, Frederick P. *Our Daily Bread.* Toronto: Macmillan, 1928.

———. *It Needs to Be Said.* Toronto: Macmillan, 1929.

———. *The Yoke of Life.* Toronto: Macmillan, 1930.

———. *Two Generations.* Toronto: Ryerson, 1939.

———. *In Search of Myself.* Toronto: Macmillan, 1946.

———. *Consider Her Ways.* Toronto: Macmillan, 1947.

———. *Over Prairie Trails.* NCL 1, 1957.

———. *The Master of the Mill.* NCL 19, 1961.

———. *Fruits of the Earth.* NCL 49, 1965.

———. *Settlers of the Marsh.* NCL 50, 1966.

Guèvremont, Germaine. *Le Survenant.* Montréal: Fides, 1962.

Haliburton, Thomas Chandler. *The Clockmaker.* NCL 6, 1958.

Harvey, Jean-Charles. *Les Demi-civilisés.* Montréal: Editions de l'homme, 1966.

Hébert, Anne. *Les Chambres de bois.* Paris: Seuil, 1958.

———. *Kamouraska.* Paris: Seuil, 1970.

Helwig, David. *The Day Before Tomorrow.* Ottawa: Oberon, 1971.

Hémon, Louis. *Maria Chapdelaine.* Paris: Livre de poche, 1954.

Hood, Hugh. *White Figure, White Ground.* Toronto: Ryerson, 1964.

———. *The Camera Always Lies.* New York: Harcourt, Brace and World, 1967.

———. *You Can't Get There from Here.* Ottawa: Oberon, 1972.

———. *The Swing in the Garden.* Ottawa: Oberon, 1975.

Horwood, Harold. *White Eskimo.* Toronto: Doubleday, 1972.

Houston, James. *The White Dawn.* New York: Harcourt Brace, 1971.

Jasmin, Claude. *La Corde au cou.* Montréal: Cercle du Livre de France, 1960.

———. *Délivrez-nous du mal.* Montréal: Editions à la page, 1961.

———. *Ethel et le terroriste.* Montréal: Déom, 1964.

———. *La Petite Patrie.* Montréal: Editions La Presse, 1972.

———. *Sainte-Adèle-la-vaisselle.* Montréal: Editions La Presse, 1974.

Joly, Richard. *Le Visage de l'attente.* Montréal: Centre de psychologie et de pédagogie, 1963.

Kirby, William. *The Golden Dog.* NCL 65, 1969.

Klein, Abraham Moses. *The Second Scroll.* NCL 22, 1961.

Knight, David. *Farquharson's Physique and What It Did to His Mind.* London: Hodder & Stoughton, 1971.

Knister, Raymond. *White Narcissus.* NCL 32, 1962.

Kreisel, Henry. *The Rich Man.* NCL 24, 1961.

———. *The Betrayal.* Toronto: McClelland and Stewart, 1964.

Kroetsch, Robert. *The Words of My Roaring.* Toronto: Macmillan, 1966.

———. *Gone Indian.* Toronto: New Press, 1973.

———. *Badlands.* Toronto: General Publishing, 1975.

Laberge, Albert. *La Scouine.* Montréal: L'Actuelle, 1972.

———. *L'Anthologie d'Albert Laberge.* Ed. Gérard Bessette. Montréal: Cercle du Livre de France, 1962.

Langevin, André. *Evadé de la nuit.* Montréal: Cercle du Livre de France, 1951.

———. *Poussière sur la ville.* Montréal: Cercle du Livre de France, 1953.

———. *Le Temps des hommes.* Montréal: Cercle du Livre de France, 1956.

———. *L'Elan d'Amérique.* Montréal: Cercle du Livre de France, 1972.

———. *Une Chaîne dans le parc.* Paris: Julliard, 1974.

Laurence, Margaret. *The Stone Angel.* NCL 59, 1965.

———. *A Jest of God.* Toronto: McClelland and Stewart, 1966.

———. *The Diviners.* Toronto: McClelland and Stewart, 1974.

Leclerc, Félix. *Carcajou.* Montréal: Editions du Jour, 1973.

Le France, Marie. *La Randonnée passionnée.* Montréal: Fides, 1962.

Lemelin, Roger. *Au pied de la pente douce.* Montréal: L'Arbre, 1948.

———. *Pierre le magnifique.* Paris: Flammarion, 1953.

———. *Les Plouffes.* Paris: Flammarion, 1955.

Le Pan, Douglas. *The Deserter.* Toronto: McClelland and Stewart, 1964.

Leprohon, Rosanna Eleanor. *The Manor House of Villerai.* Montreal: The Family Herald, 1859.

Lowry, Malcolm. *Hear Us O Lord from Heaven Thy Dwelling Place.* Philadelphia: Lippincott, 1961.

———. *Ultramarine.* Philadelphia: Lippincott, 1962.

———. *Under the Volcano.* Harmondsworth: Penguin, 1962.

———. *October Ferry to Gabriola.* New York: World, 1970.

Ludwig, Jack. *Confusions.* Toronto: McClelland and Stewart, 1963.

———. *A Woman of Her Age.* Toronto: McClelland and Stewart, 1973.

MacLennan, Hugh. *Barometer Rising.* Toronto: Collins, 1941.

———. *Two Solitudes.* Toronto: Collins, 1945.

———. *The Precipice.* Toronto: Collins, 1948.

———. *The Watch That Ends the Night.* Toronto: Macmillan, 1959.

———. *Each Man's Son.* NCL 30, 1962.

———. *Return of the Sphinx.* Toronto: Macmillan, 1967.

MacSkimming, Roy. *Formentera.* Toronto: New Press, 1972.

Maillet, Antonine. *Don l'orignal.* Montréal: Leméac, 1972.
——. *Pointe-aux-Coques.* Montréal: Leméac, 1972.
Major, André. *Le Cabochon.* Montréal: Parti Pris, 1964.
——. *La Chair de poule.* Montréal: Parti Pris, 1965.
——. *Le Vent du diable.* Montréal: Editions du Jour, 1968.
Marcotte, Gilles. *Le Poids de Dieu.* Paris: Flammarion, 1965.
——. *Retour à Coolbrook.* Paris: Flammarion, 1965.
Marlyn, John. *Under the Ribs of Death.* NCL 41, 1964.
Martin, Claire. *Doux-amer.* Montréal: Cercle du Livre de France, 1960.
——. *Quand j'aurai payé ton visage.* Montréal: Cercle du France, 1962.
McCourt, Edward. *Walk Through the Valley.* Toronto: McClelland and Stewart, 1959.
——. *Fasting Friar.* Toronto: McClelland and Stewart, 1963.
McDougall, Colin. *Execution.* Toronto: Macmillan, 1958.
Metcalf, John. *Going Down Slow.* Toronto: McClelland and Stewart, 1972.
Mitchell, W. O. *Who Has Seen the Wind.* Toronto: Macmillan, 1947.
——. *The Vanishing Point.* Toronto: Macmillan, 1973.
Moodie, Susanna. *Roughing It in the Bush.* Toronto: McClelland and Stewart, 1923. Also in NCL.
Moore, Brian. *The Luck of Ginger Coffey.* New York: Dell, 1962.
——. *The Lonely Passion of Judith Hearne.* NCL 39, 1964.
——. *I Am Mary Dunne.* Toronto: McClelland and Stewart, 1968.
Munro, Alice. *Lives of Girls and Women.* Toronto: McGraw-Hill Ryerson, 1971.
Myers, Martin. *The Assignment.* Toronto: Fitzhenry & Whiteside, 1971.
——. *Frigate.* Toronto: General Publishing, 1975.
Paradis, Suzanne. *Les Hauts Cris.* Paris: Editions de la Diaspora, 1960.
——. *Il ne faut pas sauver les hommes.* Québec: Librairie Garneau, 1961.
——. *François-les-oiseaux.* Québec: Librairie Garneau, 1967.
——. *Les Cormorans.* Québec: Librarie Garneau, 1968.
Pinsonneault, Jean-Paul. *Jérôme Aquin.* Montréal: Beauchemin, 1960.
Portal, Ellis (pseud. for Bruce Power). *Killing Ground.* Toronto: Peter Martin Associates, 1968.
Renaud, Jacques. *Le Cassé.* Montréal: Parti Pris, 1964.

Richard, Jean-Jules. *Neuf jours de haine*. Montréal: Cercle du Livre de France, 1968.

——. *Le Voyage en rond*. Montréal: Cercle du Livre de France, 1973.

Richardson, John. *Wacousta*. NCL 58, 1965.

Richler, Mordecai. *The Incomparable Atuk*. Toronto: McClelland and Stewart, 1963.

——. *Son of a Smaller Hero*. NCL 45, 1966.

——. *Cocksure*. Toronto: McClelland and Stewart, 1968.

——. *The Apprenticeship of Duddy Kravitz*. NCL 66, 1969.

——. *St. Urban's Horseman*. Toronto: McClelland and Stewart, 1971.

Ringuet (pseud. for Philippe Panneton). *Trente arpents*. Montréal: Fides, 1964.

Ross, Sinclair. *As for Me and My House*. NCL 4, 1957.

——. *Sawbones Memorial*. Toronto: McClelland and Stewart, 1974.

Roy, Gabrielle. *La Petite Poule d'eau*. Montréal: Beauchemin, 1964.

——. *Rue Deschambault*. Montréal: Beauchemin, 1964.

——. *Alexandre Chênevert*. Montréal: Beauchemin, 1964.

——. *Bonheur d'occasion*. Montréal: Beauchemin, 1965.

——. *La Montagne secrète*. Montréal: Beauchemin, 1967.

——. *La Rivière sans repos*. Montréal: Beauchemin, 1970.

——. *Cet été qui chantait*. Paris: Editions françaises, 1972.

Ryga, George. *Hungry Hills*. Toronto: Longmans, 1963.

——. *Ballad of a Stone Picker*. Toronto: Macmillan, 1966.

Sarna, Lazar. *The Man Who Lived near Nelligan*. Toronto: Coach House, 1975.

Savard, Félix-Antoine. *Menaud, maître-draveur*. Montréal: Fides, 1966.

Schroeder, Andreas. *The Late Man*. Port Clemens, B.C.: Sono Nis, 1972.

Sheldon, Michael. *The Personnel Man*. Toronto: McClelland and Stewart, 1966.

——. *The Death of a Leader*. Toronto: McClelland and Stewart, 1971.

Simard, Jean. *Mon Fils pourtant heureux*. Montréal: Cercle du Livre de France, 1956.

——. *Les Sentiers de la nuit*. Montréal: Cercle du Livre de France, 1959.

Such, Peter. *Riverrun*. Toronto: Clarke Irwin, 1973.

Sutherland, Ronald. *Lark des Neiges*. Toronto: New Press, 1971; paperback title — *The Snow Lark*. Toronto: General Publishing, 1975.

——. *Where Do the MacDonalds Bury Their Dead?* Toronto: General Publishing, 1976.

Symons, Scott. *Place d'Armes.* Toronto: McClelland and Stewart, 1967.

Tardivel, Jules-Paul. *Pour la patrie.* Montréal: La Croix, 1936.

Thériault, Yves. *La Fille laide.* Montréal: Beauchemin, 1950.

——. *Agaguk.* Québec: Institut littéraire, 1958.

——. *Ashini.* Montréal: Fides, 1960.

——. *Aaron.* Montréal: Editions de l'homme, 1965.

——. *N'Tsuk.* Montréal: Editions de l'homme, 1968.

——. *Le Dernier Havre.* Montréal: L'Actuelle, 1970.

——. *Cul de sac.* Montréal: L'Actuelle, 1970.

Thério, Adrien. *Soliloque en hommage à une femme.* Montréal: Cercle du Livre de France, 1968.

——. *La Colère du père.* Montréal: Jummonville, 1974.

Vaillancourt, Jean. *Les Canadiens errants.* Montréal: Cercle du Livre de France, 1954.

Watson, Sheila. *The Double Hook.* NCL 54, 1965.

Wiebe, Rudy. *The Temptations of Big Bear.* Toronto: McClelland and Stewart, 1973.

Wilson, Ethel. *Swamp Angel.* NCL 29, 1962.

Wiseman, Adele. *The Sacrifice.* Toronto: Macmillan, 1956.

——. *Crackpot.* Toronto: McClelland and Stewart, 1974.

Wright, Richard B. *The Weekend Man.* New York: Farrar, Straus and Giroux, 1970.

——. *In the Middle of a Life.* Toronto: Macmillan, 1973.

SECONDARY SOURCES

Atwood, Margaret. *Survival.* Toronto: Anansi, 1972.

Bergeron, Léandre. *Petit manuel d'histoire du Québec.* Montréal: Editions québécoises, 1970.

Current-Garcia, E. and Patrick, W. R. *Realism and Romanticism in Fiction.* Chicago: Scott, Foresman, 1962.

Desbiens, Jean-Paul (Frère Pierre Jérôme). *Les Insolences du Frère Untel.* Montréal: Editions de l'homme, 1960.

Dewart, Edward Hartley, ed. *Selections from Canadian Poets.* Montreal: John Lovell, 1864.

Dorsinville, Max. *Caliban Without Prospero*. Erin, Ontario: Press Porcépic, 1974.

Jones, Douglas Gordon. *Butterfly on Rock*. Toronto: University of Toronto Press, 1970.

Klinck, C. F. and Watters, R. E., eds. *Canadian Anthology*, 3rd ed. Toronto: W. J. Gage, 1974.

Klinck, C. F., ed. *Literary History of Canada*, 2nd ed. Toronto: University of Toronto Press, 1976.

Lorenz, Konrad. *On Aggression*. Tr. Marjorie Latzke. London: Methuen, 1966.

Marcotte, Gilles. *Une Littérature qui se fait*. Montréal: HMH, 1962.

Maugey, Axel. *Poésie et société au Québec*. Québec: Presses de L'Université Laval, 1972.

Moisan, Clément. *L'Age de la littérature canadienne*. Montréal: HMH, 1969.

Moss, John. *Patterns of Isolation in English-Canadian Fiction*. Toronto: McClelland and Stewart, 1974.

New, W. H. *Articulating West: Essays on Purpose and Form in Modern Canadian Literature*. Toronto: New Press, 1972.

Pacey, Desmond, ed. *The Letters of Frederick Philip Grove*. Toronto: University of Toronto Press, 1975.

Pizer, Donald. *Realism and Naturalism in Nineteenth-Century American Literature*. Carbondale: Southern Illinois University Press, 1966.

Purdy, A. W., ed. *The New Romans — Candid Canadian Opinions of the United States*. Edmonton: Hurtig, 1968.

Reich, Charles. *The Greening of America*. New York: Random House, 1970.

Sirois, Antoine. *Montréal dans le roman canadien*. Paris: Didier, 1969.

Thrall et al., eds. *A Handbook to Literature*. New York: Odyssey, 1960.

Toffler, Alvin. *Future Shock*. New York: Bantam, 1971.

Wade, Mason. *The French-Canadian Outlook*. New York: Viking, 1946.

Warwick, Jack. *The Long Journey: Literary Themes of French Canada*. Toronto: University of Toronto Press, 1968.

Weber, Max. *The Protestant Ethic and the Spirit of Capitalism*. New York: Scribner's, 1958.

Wilson, Edmund. *O Canada — An American's Notes on Canadian Culture*. London: Rupert Hart-Davis, 1967.

QUEBEC FICTION IN ENGLISH TRANSLATION

This list is mainly of novels. For lists of essays, short fiction, poetry, and other works translated into English, as well as of English-Canadian works translated into French, see "Bibliography of Canadian Books in Translation; French to English and English to French", prepared by Philip Stratford and Maureen Newman for the Committee on Translation of the Humanities Research Council of Canada, 151 Slater Street, Ottawa.

Aquin, Hubert. *Prochain épisode — Prochain Episode.* Tr. Penny Williams. Toronto: McClelland and Stewart, 1967; also in NCL.
——. *L'Antiphonaire — The Antiphonary.* Tr. Alan Brown. Toronto: Anansi, 1973.
——. *Trou de mémoire — Blackout.* Tr. Alan Brown. Toronto: Anansi, 1974.
Aubert de Gaspé, Philippe. *Les Anciens Canadiens — The Canadians of Old.* Tr. G. M. Penée. Québec: Desbarats, 1864; also *The Canadians of Old.* Tr. Charles G. D. Roberts. New York: Appleton, 1890; also *Cameron of Lochiel.* Tr. Roberts. Toronto: Copp Clark, 1905; also *Seigneur d'Haberville.* Tr. Penée. Toronto: Musson, 1929; also *Canadians of Old.* Tr. Roberts in NCL, 1974.
Beaulieu, Victory-Lévy. *Les Grand-pères — The Grandfathers.* Tr. Marc Plourde. Montreal: Harvest House, 1975.
Benoît, Jacques. *Jos Carbone — Jos Carbone.* Tr. Sheila Fischman. Montreal: Harvest House, 1975.
Bessette, Gérard. *Le Libraire — Not for Every Eye.* Tr. Glen Shortliffe. Toronto: Macmillan, 1962.
——. *L'Incubation — Incubation.* Tr. Glen Shortliffe. Toronto: Macmillan, 1967.
——. *La Bagarre — The Brawl.* Tr. Marc Lebel and Ronald Sutherland. Montreal: Harvest House, 1976.
Bosco, Monique. *La Femme de Loth — Lot's Wife.* Tr. John Glassco. Toronto: McClelland and Stewart, 1974.
Blais, Marie-Claire. *La Belle Bête — Mad Shadows.* Tr. Merloyd Lawrence. Toronto: McClelland and Stewart, 1960; also in NCL.
——. *Tête blanche — Tête Blanche.* Tr. Charles Fullman. Toronto: McClelland and Stewart, 1961; also in NCL.
——. *Le Jour est noir* and *Les Voyageurs sacrés — The Day is Dark*

and *Three Travellers.* Tr. Derek Coltman. New York: Farrar, Straus & Giroux, 1967 (includes both).

———. *Une Saison dans la vie d'Emmanuel — A Season in the Life of Emmanuel.* Tr. Derek Coltman. New York: Farrar, Straus & Giroux, 1966.

———. *David Sterne — David Sterne.* Tr. David Lobdell. Toronto: McClelland and Stewart, 1973.

———. *Manuscrits de Pauline Archange* and *Vivre! Vivre! — The Manuscripts of Pauline Archange.* Tr. Derek Coltman. New York: Farrar, Straus & Giroux, 1970 (includes both).

———. *Le Loup — The Wolf.* Tr. Sheila Fischman. Toronto: McClelland and Stewart, 1974.

———. *Un Joualonais sa joualonie — St. Lawrence Blues.* Tr. Ralph Manheim. Toronto: Doubleday, 1975.

Carrier, Roch. *La Guerre, yes sir! — La Guerre, Yes Sir!* Tr. Sheila Fischman. Toronto: Anansi, 1970.

———. *Le Deux-millième Étage — They Won't Demolish Me.* Tr. Sheila Fischman. Toronto: Anansi, 1971.

———. *Il est par là, le soleil — Is It the Sun, Philibert?* Tr. Sheila Fischman. Toronto: Anansi, 1972.

———. *Le Deux-millième Étage — They Won't Demolish Me.* Tr. Sheila Fischman. Toronto: Anansi, 1974.

Conan, Laure. *A l'oeuvre et à l'épreuve — The Master Motive.* Tr. Theresa A. Gethin. St. Louis, Mo.: Herder, 1909.

Constantin-Weyer, Maurice. *La Bourrasque — The Half-breed.* New York: Macaulay, 1930; also Toronto: Macmillan, 1930 under title *A Martyr's Folly.*

———. *Clairière — Forest Wild.* Tr. Conrad Elphinstone. London: G. Routledge, 1932.

Dantin, Louis. *Les Enfances de Fanny — Fanny.* Tr. Ray Chamberlain. Montreal: Harvest House, 1973.

Doutremont, Henri. *Nipsya — Nipsya.* Tr. Constance D. Woodrow. New York: Louis Carrier, 1929.

Ducharme, Réjean. *L'Avalée des avalés — The Swallower Swallowed.* Tr. Barbara Bray. London: Hamish Hamilton, 1968.

Elie, Robert. *La Fin des songes — Farewell My Dreams.* Tr. Irene Coffin. Toronto: Ryerson, 1954.

Ferron, Jacques. *Cotnoir — Dr. Cotnoir.* Tr. Pierre Cloutier. Montreal: Harvest House, 1973.

———. *L'Amélanchier — The Juneberry Tree.* Tr. Raymond Chamberlain. Montreal: Harvest House, 1975.

———. *Les Roses sauvages — Wild Roses.* Tr. Betty Benarski. Toronto: McClelland and Stewart, 1975.

France, Claire. *Les Enfants qui s'aiment — Children in Love.* Tr. Antonia White. Toronto: McClelland and Stewart, 1959.

Giguère, Diane. *Le Temps des jeux — Innocence.* Tr. Peter Green. Toronto: McClelland and Stewart, 1962.

———. *L'Eau est profonde — Whirlpool.* Tr. Charles Fullman. Toronto: McClelland and Stewart, 1966.

Godbout, Jacques. *Le Couteau sur la table — Knife on the Table.* Tr. Penny Williams. Toronto: McClelland and Stewart, 1968.

———. *Salut Galarneau! — Hail Galarneau.* Tr. Alan Brown. Toronto: Longmans, 1970.

Guèvremont, Germaine. *Le Survenant* and *Marie-Didace — The Outlander.* Tr. Eric Sutton. Toronto: McGraw Hill, 1950; also under title *Monk's Reach.* London: Evans Bros., 1950.

Harvey, Jean-Charles. *Les Demi-civilisés — Sackcloth for Banner.* Tr. Lukin Barrette. Toronto: Macmillan, 1938.

Hébert, Anne. *Le Torrent — The Torrent.* Tr. Gwendolyn Moore. Montreal: Harvest House, 1973.

———. *Kamouraska — Kamouraska.* Tr. Norman Shapiro. Toronto: Musson, 1973.

Hébert, Jacques. *Les Ecoeurants — The Temple on the River.* Tr. Gerald Taaffe. Montreal: Harvest House, 1967.

Hémon, Louis. *Maria Chapdelaine — Maria Chapdelaine.* Tr. W. H. Blake. Toronto: Macmillan, 1921; Tr. Andrew MacPhail. Montreal: Chapman, 1921.

Jasmin, Claude. *Ethel et le terroriste — Ethel and the Terrorist.* Tr. David S. Walker. Montreal: Harvest House, 1965.

Langevin, André. *Poussière sur la ville — Dust Over the City.* Tr. John Latrebe and Robert Gottlieb. Toronto: McClelland and Stewart, 1955; also in NCL.

Leclerc, Félix. *Allegro — Allegro.* Tr. Linda Hutcheon. Toronto: McClelland and Stewart, NCL, 1974.

LeFranc, Marie. *Grand Louis l'innocent — The Whisper of a Name.* Tr. George and Hilda Shively. Indianapolis: Bobbs-Merrill, 1928.

Lemelin, Roger. *Au pied de la pente douce — The Town Below.* Tr. Samuel Putnam. New York: Reynal & Hitchcock, 1948; also NCL.

———. *Les Plouffes — The Plouffe Family.* Tr. Mary Finch. Toronto: McClelland and Stewart, 1950.

———. *Pierre le magnifique — In Quest of Splendour.* Tr. Harry Lorne

Binsse. Toronto: McClelland and Stewart, 1955.

Marcotte, Gilles. *Le Poids de Dieu — The Burden of God.* Tr. Elizabeth Abbott. Toronto: Copp Clark, 1964; New York: Vanguard Press, 1964.

Renaud, Jacques. *Le Cassé — Flat Broke and Beat.* Tr. Gérald Robitaille. Montreal: Bélier, 1964.

Ringuet. *Trente arpents — Thirty Acres.* Tr. Felix and Dorothea Walter. Toronto: Macmillan, 1940; also in NCL.

Routhier, Adolphe-Basile. *Le Centurion — The Centurion.* Tr. Lucille P. Borden. St. Louis, Mo.: Herder, 1910.

Roy, Gabrielle. *Bonheur d'occasion — The Tin Flute.* Tr. Hannah Josephson. New York: Reynal & Hitchcock, 1947; also in NCL.

——. *La Petite Poule d'eau — Where Nests the Water Hen.* Tr. Harry Lorne Binsse. New York: Harcourt, Brace, 1951; also in NCL.

——. *Alexandre Chênevert — The Cashier.* Tr. Harry Lorne Binsse. New York: Harcourt, Brace, 1955; also in NCL.

——. *Rue Deschambault — Street of Riches.* Tr. Harry Lorne Binsse. New York: Harcourt, Brace, 1957; also in NCL.

——. *La Montagne secrète — The Hidden Mountain.* Tr. Harry Lorne Binsse. Toronto: McClelland and Stewart, 1961; also in NCL.

——. *La Route d'Altamont — The Road Past Altamont.* Tr. Joyce Marshall. Toronto: McClelland and Stewart, 1966.

——. *La Rivière sans repos — Windflower.* Tr. Joyce Marshall. Toronto: McClelland and Stewart, 1970.

Savard, Félix-Antoine. *Menaud, maître-draveur — Boss of the River.* Tr. Alan Sullivan. Toronto: Ryerson, 1947.

Thériault, Yves. *Agaguk — Agaguk.* Tr. Miriam Chapin. Toronto: Ryerson, 1963.

——. *Ashini — Ashini.* Tr. Gwendolyn Moore. Montreal: Harvest House, 1972.

——. *N'Tsuk — N'Tsuk.* Tr. Gwendolyn Moore. Montreal: Harvest House, 1971.

Vigneault, Gilles. *Contes sur la pointe des pieds — Tales (Sur la Pointe des Pieds).* Tr. Paul Allard. Erin, Ont.: Porcépic, 1972.

Index